SCHOLAS

GRAMMAR LESSONS
YOU'LL LOVE TO TEACH

Highly Motivating Lessons—With Pizzazz—That Help Kids
Become More Effective Readers, Writers, and Thinkers

Ruth Townsend Story
and
Cathleen F. Greenwood

New York • Toronto • London • Auckland • Sydney
Mexico City • New Delhi • Hong Kong • Buenos Aires **Teaching** *Resources*

DEDICATION

*To our students, who have always been our inspiration and motivation, and
to our husbands, sons, and daughters, who have always told us to go for it.*

ACKNOWLEDGMENTS

Our approach to the teaching and learning of grammar is made possible by the many fine teachers, writers, and researchers whose work has informed and motivated us to make the teaching and learning of grammar relevant, and rewarding.

We are especially indebted . . .

to Nancie Atwell and Linda Rief for showing us why and how to put student workshop pedagogy at the heart of the reading and writing classroom.

to Martha Kolln, Harry Noden, Rei Noguchi, and Constance Weaver
for their research into the teaching of grammar.

to Kenneth Koch, William Stafford, Stephen Dunning, and Georgia Heard
for showing us how to make poetry come alive.

to Donald Graves for all he does to support teachers and students,
and especially for his book, *Testing Is Not Teaching* (Heinemann, 2002).

to Rippowam Cisqua School in Bedford, NY, especially Kathleen McNamara, the principal who said, "Definitely—knock your lights out!" when the permission for a Grammar and Snacks Club was first sought; and Jihad Mirza and Jennifer Millett-Barrett in the Development Office with Tim Coffey, photographer, for providing the wonderful photos that accompany our text.

to Scholastic, especially David Goddy, Vice President, Terry Cooper, Editor-in-Chief, and Joanna Davis-Swing, Editorial Director, for their belief in and support of our work; and especially to Merryl Maleska Wilbur, Development and Project Editor, who worked tirelessly to shape and hone this book.

Without the support and encouragement of these fine people, this book could not have been written.

We also thank the following people who read and responded to the book in helpful and positive ways: Leila Christenbury, Virginia Commonwealth University, Richmond, VA; Kim Ford, Cypress Junior High School, Tennessee, and Department Editor, *Voices from the Middle* (NCTE); Victor Jaccarino, Department Chair of English, Herricks High School, Long Island, NY; Carol Jago, Santa Monica High School, and California Reading and Literature Project UCLA; Linda Rief, Oyster River Middle School, Durham, NH, and Department Editor, *Voices from the Middle* (NCTE); Kate Dunlop Seamans, Editor, *Teen Ink;* Joe Trimmer, Virginia Ball Center for Creative Inquiry, Ball State University, Muncie, IN; Joanne Yatvin, NCTE Vice President, Portland State University, Portland, OR.

CREDITS

Poem (p. 98) by Sam Sacks, "Learning a Language," words from PREPARATORY LATIN BOOK I,
Second edition; poem reprinted from SO, YOU WANNA BE A WRITER by permission of Beyond Words Publishing.

Excerpt (p. 100) from *Defenders of Wildlife* magazine (Summer 2005), Defenders of Wildlife,
1130 17th Street, NW, Wash DC

Scholastic Inc. grants teachers permission to reproduce student reproducibles in this book for classroom use only. No other part of this publication may be reproduced in whole or in part, or stored in a retrieval system, or transmitted in any form or by any means, electronic, mechanical, photocopying, recording, or otherwise, without written permission of the publisher. For information regarding permission, write to Scholastic Inc., 557 Broadway, New York, NY 10012.

Cover design by Jaime A. Lucero
Interior design by Solutions by Design, Inc.
Cover photos, top row, l to r: Maria Lilja; © Comstock Images; Jimmy Levin/Studio 10;
bottom row, l to r: © Yellow Dog Productions/Getty Images; Jimmy Levin/Studio 10
Interior photos courtesy of the authors.

ISBN: 0-439-70070-1

Copyright © 2006 by Ruth Townsend Story and Cathleen F. Greenwood. All rights reserved. Published by Scholastic Inc.
Printed in the U.S.A.

4 5 6 7 8 9 10   40   12 11 10

TABLE OF CONTENTS

Becoming a Teacher of Grammar

*Grammar is a piano I play by ear.
All I know about grammar is its power.*

—Joan Didion

Grammar Power

THERE THEY ARE: A ROOMFUL OF STUDENTS IMPLICITLY challenging you to engage them, stimulate them, and maybe even teach them something they want to learn. You know what they need to learn: to become skillful readers, writers, and speakers. But as an English teacher, you also know for that to happen you have to hook them on language, make it fun to play with, easy to learn, relevant in their lives. Let's face it. You have to make the study of the way our language works—that is, *grammar*—something they want

to learn. So you plunge in, eager to share your love of language and your enthusiasm for grammar with them.

"Who wants to be a millionaire?" you ask your class.

All hands go up. "Me!" "I do!" "Oh, yeah!" they respond.

"Who wants to be a rock star or an Olympic gold medal winner?" Same enthusiastic response.

Then you ask, "Who wants to be a grammarian?" Raised eyebrows, a few titters, a question or two: "A what?"

"A grammarian," you repeat.

"Is that some kind of animal trainer?" one student asks. You hope she is just kidding.

"So," you ask, "what do you imagine you get by being a millionaire, or a rock star, or a gold medal winner?"

You can be sure someone will say, "Lots of money . . . and lots of power." And since money is a kind of power, he or she will be right.

Then you tell the class that a grammarian is also a kind of power broker—in this case, a person who understands how language works and so has control over how he or she uses the language. You go on to explain that you want them to have that kind of power. With grammar power they can write and speak to explain clearly, argue convincingly, describe vividly; they can even read with deeper understanding and insight. Few of us will ever be millionaires, or rock stars, or winners of Olympic gold medals, but all of us can learn to be grammarians and exercise our power of language.

Our approach to teaching grammar is something we call "grammar goodness." In the land of grammar goodness, we put our students in charge of their own learning, setting each off on a discovery process to find out what grammar knowledge can do for them as writers, readers, and speakers. Along the way, we support them as coaches, helping them acquire the grammar knowledge that makes them stronger readers and more effective writers and speakers. Our challenge is to meet students wherever they are in their grammar needs, so that the grammar curriculum is determined by their use of language; in effect, student reading, writing, and speaking must determine what grammar is taught and how it is taught.

To integrate that teaching into the total curriculum, we need to have at the ready a bank of grammar expertise and solid lessons and activities to pull out for teachable moments. This book is designed to help you enrich your bank of grammar goodness and empower you to share it with your students.

What Is Grammar, Anyway?

Grammar, in broad terms, is the science of language. But in practice, it is the art of correct use of language according to grammatical rules that affect pronunciation, inflection, and syntax. In other words, grammar describes the way our language works in allowing us to communicate, to create, and, most important, to relate as one human being to another. So it stands to reason that the better we understand the working of our language, the better able we are to use it—the more power we have with it. Our students have the right to know how to use the power of language to communicate for a variety of purposes and audiences—and not only *how*, but how to do it *well*, which means they need to know:

- Parts of speech
- Rules of usage
- Patterns of words
- Structures of sentences
- Arrangement of sentences

But please be careful. We are trusting that you will not use this book to teach grammar the way many of us were taught: as justification for giving quizzes on grammar rules, adding grades to the grade book, using a red pen liberally, preparing for standardized tests, or intimidating young learners. The goal of good grammar teaching is to stimulate thinking, promote questioning, and encourage experimentation, thus enabling students to use language consciously and confidently in all kinds of "real life" situations.

Now, Honestly—Do We Really Need to Teach Grammar?

R EALISTICALLY, WE KNOW STUDENTS ARE NOT GOING TO LEARN Standard English, the language of power, on their own unless that is the English they regularly hear in their personal lives, both at home and with their friends. Not a likely situation for many American children.

By the time students reach our classrooms, they have picked up a good deal of their grammar from TV and movies, the Internet, blogs, friends, older siblings—you get the idea. They also deserve to learn it from their teachers, who can give them the tools to put what they know—and will know—to work for them as writers, readers, and speakers, not just for success in school but in the workplace. Now we must acknowledge that some very successful people butcher the English language in the "real world." Whether or not they use the "rules" doesn't seem to matter. So we can't pretend to our students that unless they know grammar rules they have no hope of economic success. But what we can tell them is that if they want a fair, reasonable chance for success in today's world, they deserve to learn to shift from home talk to school talk to workplace talk as the need arises.

The ability to use language effectively and correctly according to the rules of Standard English empowers us personally and professionally. The truth is that people are judged by the way they use language. And the more knowledge our students have of the structure of language and the effect of those structures on readers and listeners, the better able they are to decide how to use language at home, with friends, in school, and in the workplace.

They may consciously choose to break the rules, create new structures, or adapt the language for their audience. And that's as it should be. When they are manipulating their language by making informed choices, they contribute to the evolutionary development of the English language as a whole. We want them to be able to do that. We believe that kind of grammar power is their right. But, just as firmly, we believe that their having the basic correct information in the first place is the springboard for all else.

Okay, So What's the Best Way to Teach Grammar Without Scaring Them Off?

FOR STUDENTS TO IDENTIFY AND YOU TO ASSESS THEIR GRAMMAR needs, you need a system. But that's just the first step, as you'll see when we share our system with you in Part II. Then you must teach them what they need to know about the grammar of English. But how? you ask. Let's consider what does *not* work:

- ⑥ Memorizing definitions of parts of speech
- ⑥ Out-of-context worksheets
- ⑥ Out-of-context sentence diagramming
- ⑥ Frequent quizzes
- ⑥ Fill-in-the-blank tests
- ⑥ Red-lining student papers

Oh, sure, some students will learn enough to do well on these kinds of activities, but the real measure of learning is the extent to which that learning is internalized and applied to their reading, writing, and speaking, both in and out of the classroom. Based on our experience reading students' writing, assessing their reading comprehension, and listening to them speak, we believe there is little or no carryover from those kinds of classroom activities to applied practice.

So what does work? you want to know.

We believe that grammar has to be taught in the context of our English language system. Lynn Sams (2003) argues this point convincingly in her article "How to Teach Grammar, Analytical Thinking, and Writing: A Method That Works." Sams contends that to teach grammar as an isolated set of rules, ignoring the context from which the rules derive, the language itself, is an exercise in futility. That's certainly been our experience. Because so few of our students have any background knowledge about grammar, or grammatical concepts, or even a grammar vocabulary, we are, as Sams puts it, "attempting to teach grammar in a vacuum." We agree.

Our approach is to integrate direct language instruction with reading, writing, and speaking instruction. We do this by:

- ⑥ Engaging students in composing activities that involve them in the vocabulary of grammar and in exploring the relationship between words, phrases, clauses, and sentences and the products they are creating.
- ⑥ Exploring models of good writing to see how professional writers use language, first focusing on specific grammar topics (e.g., diction, verb

Grammar Lessons You'll Love to Teach Scholastic Teaching Resources

choices, sentence beginnings, sentence variety, even punctuation), and then having them put these tools of the craft to work in their own writing.

- ⑥ Inviting students to listen to people speaking in school (yes, even the teachers and administrators), at home, in the community, on the radio and television, and in the movies to raise their awareness of the relationship between grammar and communication.

- ⑥ Examining the language of the Internet, popular magazines, tabloids, newspapers, advertising, fund-raising brochures, community publications, and even school communications to analyze the effect of diction, syntax, and usage on the reader.

- ⑥ Encouraging students to take charge of their language power and grammar goodness by reflecting on their own speaking and writing, targeting areas for growth, and setting personal goals for progress.

A note about the final point above. You'll find that virtually all the reproducibles in this book include answer keys. We do this deliberately so that students are empowered while practicing. This provides them with immediate feedback and frees them from having to wait for the "expert" to correct or confirm whether they are on the right track. Nor do students have to worry that the practice pages are going to be used for grades. As well, teachers save time by not correcting or going over all the answers in class; they can use that class time instead to address the questions that students identify on their own as problematic. Giving students answers is a fairly unique concept in grammar books. As we see it, trust is an integral part of grammar goodness. We trust our students' desire to learn so much that we give them the tools that the experts use.

But Do I Have Time for This?

Of course you do. You're already teaching language when you focus on reading, writing, and speaking in your classroom. So all you need to do is build into your reading, writing, and speaking activities appropriate lessons on the structure and use of language. You don't have to teach a whole book of grammar. In fact, don't even *think* about doing that.

Instead, take a thorough look at the Table of Contents for this book. Try to reconceptualize grammar lessons within a context that's actually fun for both you and your students (such as the Grammar and Snacks Club described in Part I). Then become familiar with the "System" detailed in Part II, especially with the Decoder List and the Personal Skills Record. Before you know it, we bet you'll start to feel comfortable with correcting writing by using just the skills codes in margins. Then you'll start noticing the most common skills students are missing (and by the way, they will start noticing, too).

The next step will be to find lessons that focus on those particular skills (in Parts III and IV) and start teaching to those issues, choosing the lessons and activities in this book that you think will work for your students. You may end up supplementing with extra practice and workbook pages from your book closet; this is fine, of course, as long as you remember that the objective is to keep the grammar learning focused on what students need in order to grow in their own reading and writing. And, finally, rather than spending hours grading grammar in situations that don't truly require grades, you can refer to our assessment guide (Part V) for advice.

Grammar Goodness for Life

REMEMBER: THINK OF YOURSELF AS A COACH WHOSE TASK IS TO ENABLE students to take charge of their own learning—the kind that stays with them long after they leave the classroom. For life.

We will guide you through the system, the direct teaching methods we use, the integrated composing and writing techniques that have worked for us. We will recommend resources that will give you hands-on help, and direct you to Web sites for information, ideas, and encouragement so that you can successfully share your grammar goodness with your students.

And throughout it all, we urge you to keep in mind the history of the definition of *grammar:*

> *grammar:* . . . In the Middles Ages, *grammatica* and its Roman forms chiefly meant the knowledge or study of Latin; and were hence often used as synonymous with learning in general, the knowledge peculiar to the learned class. As this was popularly supposed to include **magic** and astrology O.F. *gramaire* was sometimes used as a name for these occult sciences. In these applications, it still survives in certain corrupt forms, F. *grimoire,* Eng/Scottish. **glamour.***
>
> **Oxford English Dictionary, Second Edition. Prepared by J.A.Simpson and E.S.C. Weiner. Oxford, GB: Clarendon Press. 1989. Volume VI, p. 742.*

In the end, we hope you'll agree that grammar can indeed be glamorous magic!

PART I

Establishing the Context

It is grammar, first of all, that makes language possible, that allows us to articulate our thought, our selves, in utterances.

—Oliver Sacks

THEY'VE GOT TO WANT IT.

It was a dark and stormy Wednesday. The study hall door shot open and Nick's voice rang out: "I am here to talk about run-on sentences. Once and for all."

We wish we could say that at that moment the clouds parted, rays of sunshine streamed through the windows, and seraphim sang out on high, but of course they didn't. Instead, we experienced brain freeze at the magnitude of the moment: *Now we've got him. But are we up to this? He wants to know, once and for all. Can we keep him going—now and forever?*

We had tried so many methods—grammar workbooks, quizzes, points off for every mistake, "Yes, grammar counts every time" speeches, extra credit, make-up tests, peer edits (ouch)—and their papers bled with red ink, their writing became stilted and bruised, and everyone hated grammar and said they stunk at it. Stunk.

We knew we had to find some new approaches . . ..

The Grammar and Snacks Club

How We Got From There to Here: A True Story

Sometimes desperation, rather than necessity, is the mother of invention for teachers. So it was with the Grammar and Snacks Club. Early attempts at teaching grammar resulted in moans, blank stares, and window gazing. From those few students who chose to participate, calling-out shouting contests erupted as wild guesses were made. Random grammar-related words were bandied about: *Noun! Semicolon! Comma splice! Business letter! Gerund!* Nonsense reigned. It was like having a classroom full of Peppermint Patties, along with a few Bart Simpsons, multiplied many times. Pupils were convinced that grammar was impossible. Boring. Evil. Useless. Nothing was learned. Teachers were miserable. There was no Grammar Goodness in the land.

The Grammar and Snacks Club opened for business, offering Hershey's chocolate Kisses to potential members. Grammar lessons, writing conferences, and extra help sessions were renamed Grammar and Snacks Club meetings. The teacher morphed into Head Pro/Coach. Snacks (a Hershey's Kiss for each) were offered at the start and end of each meeting. There were practice sessions with plenty of practice, and "games" (quizzes and tests) scheduled in advance. Pre- and post-game snacks were provided. There was even an end-of-term Member Guest Tournament; the invitation was the hottest item in school. Prizes were Mad Libs (the grammar piece) and M&M's (the snacks piece).

Now the classroom was a happy place. Students were learning and teachers were smiling. Grammar Goodness ruled.

A Few Ground Rules for Getting Started

As most of us are aware, a name can connote a concept or a feeling well beyond its literal meaning. This can be especially true for intermediate-grade students, who are extremely sensitive to social and contextual nuances. Call something a "class" and it means one thing, call it a "club" and it's a whole different ball game. Mention grammar on its own and you'll probably hear the fabled groans described above. Link grammar to something extremely pleasant, like snacks, and you may encounter an unexpected receptiveness.

And so we suggest that you try to establish the context (or your own variation) that has worked miraculously for us: Whenever you teach grammar (whether in class or in a student conference or extra-help session), proclaim that the Grammar and Snacks Club is having a meeting, and distribute a Hershey's Kiss or to each student (snacks come first). After all, as in any club, membership in the Grammar and Snacks Club has its status, privileges, and perks. The moans will stop when grammar rears its (now positive) head. The next time you announce a meeting, you might actually hear some cheers!

Materials and supplies for the club are easy. Here's all you'll need:

- **Hershey's Kisses or other snacks.** Incidentally, and this is important given our nation's growing awareness of children's eating habits: The snack doesn't have to be nutritionally challenged or sugar laden—you can use pretzel rods, cinnamon apple chips, or other healthy alternatives.

Note: If you teach in a school that does not allow food distribution in the classroom, you might implement instead a gold star sticker system on a club membership chart or book.

- **A straightforward framework or system within which you present instruction.** Ours incorporates our Personal Skills Record, a modified version of Nancie Atwell's well-known Skills List, and our own Decoder List, student-friendly descriptions of key skills. As part of this system, students grow their own lists of targeted skills based on the mistakes they make in their own writing and they copy one skill rule each time they misuse it. (See Part II for a full description of the System.)

- **Grammar lesson materials based on what you plan to teach, grammar workbook page handouts, and so on.** (See Parts III and IV for specific lesson plans and ideas.)

- **A simple assessment and evaluation guide.** (See Part V for the one we recommend.)

As you set up your club, let students in on your goals. Our own goals were quite simple and basic:

- To acknowledge students' assumptions, anxieties, feelings of being stupid, and just plain anger over learning grammar in school, and instead offer humor, a sense of belonging, and confidence.

- To allow all students a fresh start in learning grammar, eliminating all assumptions of what was taught or learned in the past.

- To offer young people the chance to say they are learning grammar as part of a "club" rather than as part of a mandatory class. (Naturally, this club meets during mandatory class time, or extra-help time, but it is still for Members Only; only the Grammar-Challenged need apply—which of course, includes everyone.)

- To give a student an excuse to smile when grammar is mentioned, or the chance to claim that he or she is coming for extra help or participating in grammar class because "I just came for the snack."

Welcome students to each class/session as you would welcome members to any club, and act the role of proud president and head coach. Treat your members as you would treat new members in a soccer club or tennis club, letting them see how pleased you are that they have joined. As their pro and coach, promise to help them learn and improve at their own pace. Make sure you tell them that you know they can learn grammar, but you understand that sometimes it takes instruction and practice, just as it does in tennis or soccer. We recommend having students sign a special club membership form, such as the Member Guidelines for Grammar Goodness reproducible on page 17, which spells out club member responsibilities and expectations.

It's important to explain why you have chosen a specific topic for each "club meeting" and how it will help students "improve their game." For example, you might say, "Today we will be working on comma splices because I noticed a lot of you have to copy that rule onto your Personal Skills Record. [Note: The Personal Skills Record is presented and described in Part II.] I'm sure you would like to be able to stop making the same mistake over and over—and copying that darn rule! Also, learning about comma splices will help those of you who might be having problems with run-ons or fragments." We have found it helpful to distribute an informal lesson plan, which we call our Meeting Agenda Planner, at the start of each lesson (see page 18). Having a form like this in hand helps students feel like they are an active part of the club meeting.

Use your teaching devices to support the club. For example, we use the Preposition Song, sung to the tune of "Pop Goes the Weasel," as our club song (see page 19). Students love the silliness, and at the same time they're painlessly picking up grammar basics. The same logic lies behind our Grammar and Snacks Club Cheers (see page 20). Punctuating accented syllables with pumping fists or even pompoms, we (along with volunteers) cheer, "The *ob*ject of a *prep*osition *al*ways takes ob*jec*tive case," and "The *verb* 'to be' always takes sub*jec*tive case." Feel free to start and end meetings with a song or cheer—or both.

Encourage members to become actively involved in the club's success by helping them to understand their particular learning styles and by playing up the importance of their roles as members. Here are some ways to do this:

- Take regular polls of your members on lesson topics, and on the effectiveness of various teaching strategies, books, and handouts.

- If you have a variety of grammar books gathering dust in the book closet, spend a class session having students work in small groups to evaluate them for selection as club materials.

- Set up coaching sessions that are headed by students who have mastered certain skills; both the member who is helping others and the student whose skills are improving will feel more involved in the club.

- Make time for students to tell grammar stories at the start of each meeting. These stories might include grammar mistakes noticed in the media or everyday life; celebrations of personal progress noticed by a member ("I didn't have any comma splice errors in my last Teacher Edit!"); or sharing of strategies that worked for a particular student ("Jamie told me this trick to remember how to spell *separate*: There is A RAT in sepA RATe.")

You don't need to limit the Grammar and Snacks Club meetings to regular class time. Whenever you have a writing conference with a student, consider it also a Grammar and Snacks Club meeting and bring out the Hershey's Kisses and other goodies. This goes, as well, for any extra-help session that might remotely touch on grammar.

It's fun to run practice drills as team challenges or doubles contests. Create teams or student pairs and have appropriate questions ready on the overhead. Uncover the questions one at a time. Call on teams in clockwise (or any other specified) order and award a team a poker chip for getting an answer correct. In the case of an incorrect answer, allow the next team to earn a poker chip by giving the correct answer *and* a complete explanation. At the end of the game, give prizes to the teams with the most poker chips—a special snack, or even a Mad Libs book along with the snack if it's a big tournament. Be a sport—offer second and third place prizes, too.

Grammar Lessons You'll Love to Teach Scholastic Teaching Resources

Use this same format for end-of-term member-guest tournaments (see page 21). Students may invite one guest—anyone in the school, including a teacher or administrator. Warning: These events can become so popular that you might have to schedule them after school!

Eventually, students might really get into the club idea and want to take on executive board roles. Rejoice in their willingness to take ownership. Kids can have fun bringing in snacks, helping to take attendance, creating membership cards, voting on lesson topics, leading the club song and cheers, organizing games and tournaments—and all the while, take secret pride in holding office in the Grammar and Snacks Club.

It's Okay to Use (Kid-Friendly) Grammar Texts and Books

In choosing grammar materials, remember two key concepts. The first is that there is no need to reinvent the wheel. There are plenty of good books already out there. If you try to invent your own exercises, you'll almost certainly find yourself on a slippery slope fraught with the perils of explaining gerunds or subjective case with the verb *to be* when all you wanted to do was have the students identify prepositional phrases.

The second concept to bear in mind is that the "no pain, no gain" axiom should not be part of a grammar goodness game plan. Studies have shown that laughter releases endorphins in the brain that allow us to learn better. In addition, it is a basic principle of human nature that we want to repeat what is pleasurable for us, and avoid what is not. Lighten up, let learning happen with time and humor, and grammar goodness will abound.

You and your students deserve a grammar text with concise and clear definitions of grammar terms and rules. The text should not be boring. It should include examples that appeal to learners at appropriate grade levels. For instance, look for examples that use material present in other disciplines for that grade level (such as sample sentences that tell the life story of Madame Curie) or that incorporate popular cultural references (such as to *The Lord of the Rings* or Harry Potter). Look, too, for humor—most middle-school and early teen students respond to genuine humor and appreciate the chance to mix laughing and learning.

Of course, we realize that there are times (no time to order!) or situations (budget!) in which you may need to resort to the set of Warriner's or other writing handbooks or style guides that are sitting in the back of the school book closet. There is little humor in these kinds of standard textbooks, but the explanations are clear and concise, and there are plenty of exercises. Keep a few of these old stand-bys (or a class set, if you have one) in your room. Use them for quick reference and as a source for exercises as the need arises. Don't feel pressured to "cover" all the chapters—just pick and choose topics and activities according to your students' needs.

You will also need a workbook that is age appropriate and enjoyable so that students have the chance to (relatively painlessly) practice new concepts and skills, as well as review old ones. Good practice sentences should meet the same criteria described above:

connections to grade-level disciplines, pop culture, or humor. Practice pages with answer keys are extremely important.

We are firm believers in practice. One lesson, even one excellently taught lesson, does not grammar goodness make. Can you imagine if you tried to play a round of golf or a violin concerto after only one lesson? Our goal is to empower students to apply grammar, usage, punctuation, and spelling skills on their own, but they need and deserve time to practice and really learn these skills before they have to play in a match—or take a test, or submit writing for corrections.

The list below contains our current favorite grammar guides. Check the bibliography at the end of this book for a detailed description of each book.

1. *Nitty-Gritty Grammar: A Not-So-Serious Guide to Clear Communication* and *More Nitty-Gritty Grammar: Another Not-So-Serious Guide to Clear Communication.* (Berkeley, CA: Ten Speed Press, 1998; 2001)

2. *Exercises in English: Grammar for Life* (Chicago: Loyola Press, 2003.)

3. *Grammar Smart* (*Princeton Review*), 2nd edition. (New York, NY: Random House, 2001.)

4. *Laugh Your Way Through Grammar* (New York, NY: Amsco School Publications, 1990.)

5. *Grammar Lessons and Strategies That Strengthen Students' Writing, Grades 4-8.* (New York, NY: Scholastic Inc., 2001.)

Member Guidelines for Grammar Goodness

1. I accept that grammar goodness is made, not born, and that it will increase with attention, instruction, and practice.

2. If I do not know how a specific grammar skill or lesson will improve my reading, writing, or speaking, I must ask.

3. For the convenience of club members, the term grammar may be used in reference to spelling, punctuation, and word usage, as well as traditional grammar terms and principles.

4. I will do practice pages to the best of my ability before checking the answer keys.

5. I am not a Grammar Cop. When I hear someone make a grammar mistake, I will not correct him or her. Instead, I will smile a smile of serenity, radiate silent grammar goodness vibes, and make a note to discuss the issue at the next Grammar and Snacks Club meeting. I will keep the offender's name anonymous.

6. I will keep a running record of my grammar errors in my Personal Skills Record.

7. I will use my Personal Skills Record to help me revise and edit before submitting any piece of writing.

8. I will review my grammar goodness progress on a regular basis, and share improvements and successful strategies at Grammar and Snacks Club meetings.

9. During Grammar and Snacks Club meetings, challenge sessions, or team play, I will:

   a. Take time to think before giving an answer.

   b. Raise my hand instead of simply calling out answers.

   c. Wait at least 30 seconds before calling on a raised hand if I am acting as the Grammar and Snacks Club leader.

Member signature _____

Date _____

Meeting Agenda Planner for _____ (date)

(Check items planned for this date.)

____ **I.** Call to order with snack distribution.

____ **II.** Club Cheer

        a. Cheer #1: "The object of a preposition always takes objective case."

        b. Cheer #2: " The verb *to be* always takes subjective case."

____ **III.** Club Song: "The Preposition Song"

____ **IV.** Review "Member Guidelines for Grammar Goodness"

____ **V.** Members share grammar stories:

        a. Personal improvements or successful strategies

        b. Grammar mistakes noted in everyday life

____ **VI.** Today's grammar topic: _____

        a. How learning today's topic will help members to increase their grammar goodness in their reading and writing

        _____

        b. Materials for direct instruction on grammar topic

        _____

        _____

        c. Practice pages with answer keys and group review of problem questions

        _____

        _____

        d. Closing challenge session in groups or pairs

____ **VII.** Closing (use one or more):

        a. Snack

        b. Club Song

        c. Cheer #1: "The object of a preposition always takes objective case."

        d. Cheer #2: " The verb *to be* always takes subjective case."

Official Song: The Preposition Song

(Note: The words to "Pop Goes the Weasel" are included here only to help demonstrate the tune of "The Preposition Song" and are not intended to be sung.)

VERSE 1:

All around the mulberry bush
about above across after

the monkey chased the weasel
against among around

the monkey thought it was all in fun—
at before beside between

POP goes the weasel.
by down during

VERSE 2:

A penny for a spool of thread;
except for from in into

a penny for a needle,
near of off on over

That's the way the money goes—
through to toward under

POP goes the weasel.
up with within without

Grammar and Snacks Club Cheers

One member leads the cheer first, then all members join in.

Put emphasis and pause on underlined syllables when announcing cheers.

Repeat each cheer at least three times.

Use before, during, and/or after each club meeting.

CHEER #1: The <u>ob</u>ject of a <u>prep</u>osition <u>al</u>ways takes ob<u>jec</u>tive case.

Purpose: This cheer helps members to remember to use the objective case for pronouns in prepositional phrases.

Example: *Harry learned the spell with Ron and her.* (not *with Ron and she*)

Explanation: The pronoun *her* is the object of the preposition *with* and must therefore be objective case.

Example: *Mom, Jimmy threw the snake at Billy and me!* (not *at Billy and I*)

Explanation: Because *me* is the object of the preposition *at*, it must be objective case.

CHEER #2: The <u>verb</u> *to <u>be</u>* always takes <u>subj</u>ective case.

Purpose: This cheer helps members to remember to use the subjective case for pronouns used with the verb *to be* (predicate nominatives and subject complements).

Example: He-Who-Must-Not-Be-Named has done this awful deed. It is he! (not *It is him!*)

Explanation: The verb *is*, which is a form of the verb *to be*, takes the subjective case.

Example: "Are you looking for Hermione?" she asked. "You have found her. I am she." (not *I am her*)

Explanation: The verb *am*, which is a form of the verb *to be*, takes the subjective case.

Note: To use these cheers and put grammar goodness to work in your life, you need to know:

1. Pronoun cases:

   Subjective case: I, you, he, she, it, we, you, they, who

   Objective case: me, you, him, her, it, us, you, them, whom

2. The verb *to be* in its magical forms:

I am	we are	I was	we were
you are	you are	you were	you were
he/she/it/who is	they are	he/she/it/who was	they were
I have been	we have been	I will be	we will be
you have been	you have been	you will be	you will be
he/she/it/who has been	they have been	he/she/it/who will be	they will be

Grammar Lessons You'll Love to Teach Scholastic Teaching Resources

Invitation to Member-Guest Tournament

Grammar and Snacks Club Member

_____
(member name)

cordially invites

_____
(guest name)

to the
Grammar and Snacks Club
Member-Guest Tournament

Date: _____

Time: _____ to _____

Location: _____

Snacks and Prizes will be provided.
Please bring this invitation with you for admittance.

PART II

Setting Up the System

*It is well to remember that grammar is
common speech formulated.*

—William Somerset Maugham

Remember Nick from Part I? He wanted to solve the run-on sentences mystery "once and for all." Armed with motivation and inspiration to respond to him and his legions of grammar-weary peers, we not only established the Grammar and Snacks Club but we also developed the System, the instructional backbone of the club. The System is a cohesive, integrated approach that doesn't take over your curriculum but enhances your teaching and empowers students to be effective communicators. It is driven by what students really need (as demonstrated in their own writing), not by the calendar or someone else's ideas about students' needs.

This section provides three lessons that you can use to introduce this system to your students. It also includes a Decoder List of correction symbols and rules and a Personal Skills Record that students will develop all year to target their grammar needs.

To *awk* or Not to *awk*: Correcting With Codes and a Decoder List

INTRODUCTION

Do you remember the first time you saw those weird words like *awk* or *frag,* probably written in red pen or pencil, in the margins of your papers? Did you have any idea what they meant? Did your teacher make you look them up in Warriner's, even though you could not find them in a dictionary? When you finally found out what they meant, did that even help your writing? Chances are, the results were feelings ranging from confusion and frustration to embarrassment or anger, and perhaps eventually to resignation. Chances are, too, that not many of your classmates rushed up to the teacher and thanked her. Instead, they probably trudged home to make the corrections as quickly as they could in order to submit the corrected paper—actually corrected by the teacher, mind you—back to the teacher.

As we see it, red-lining papers as a way of teaching grammar and punctuation is not a very effective way to help students learn to become better writers. Teachers who red-line—simply use a red pen to correct and/or use correction codes—help students make required corrections, for sure, but no real learning is happening. Too often, teachers who simply "correct" student writing are really only providing a form of free proofreading.

Of course, we must help students to see and understand their errors, but we also need to teach ways and means for students themselves to correct their work, to learn from their mistakes, and so to improve their writing on an ongoing basis. Thus, we believe it makes sense to establish a list of rules and skills with accompanying codes or abbreviations for students' own quick use when correcting. We call it the Decoder List (see pages 31–37).

In the first months of the school year, we correct students' work, using codes in the margins and building actual corrections directly into their writing. After the first months, we simply use the codes. But from the beginning, students' first task upon receipt of a corrected paper is to look up the codes in their Decoder List, and then to copy each targeted skill into their Personal Skills Record (see pages 38–39). Although we may eventually give a progress grade at the end of each term, based on evidence of learning in the Personal Skills Record, we don't give any grades in the beginning. We just make the necessary corrections and add positive comments wherever we can. The primary task at this point is to pay attention to the most common mistakes, and make a list of, say, the top five to use to generate future lessons.

What students need to know and be able to do:

⊚ Become familiar with a user-friendly list of the grammar and usage rules and skills most commonly needed by middle and high school writers, with accompanying codes commonly used by teachers and editors

⊚ Start an individual Personal Skills Record, an ongoing list of grammar and usage skills generated from mistakes encountered in the student's own writing

....
MATERIALS
....

⊚ One photocopy for each student of the Decoder List (pages 31–37)

⊚ Overhead transparency of the Decoder List

⊚ One photocopy for each student of the Personal Skills Record (page 39)

⊚ Overhead transparency of the Skills Record/Student Sample (page 38)

Instructional Suggestions

1 Invite students to list ways that they make use of a teacher's corrections to their written work. Write these on the board. The list might include "Look for the grade"; "Ask my mother what this means"; "Make corrections on computer and print and resubmit"; "Come for extra help"; "Ask my friend what something means."

2 If no one has included it, add this to the list described above: "Ask for suggestions on how I can avoid making the same mistakes in future writing." Elicit what specific activities these suggestions might comprise. Some might include "Reread old papers"; "Remember my old mistakes"; "Ask my father to correct it before I hand it in." Discuss how practical or realistic these kinds of activities really are—for example, will kids really search out and read over their old papers when revising new ones, and how well do students really learn if they're relying on someone else to find mistakes?

3 Explain that today you will be giving them a Decoder List that will help them decode the corrections in their writing. The list is a big one, but they will not have to learn all of the rules at once—only the ones that they need to focus on in a particular piece of writing.

4 On the board, draw two vertical lines to indicate a margin, and to the right of this "margin" write the following sentence:

Ivan had six pets, an iguana, two dogs, a parrot, a guinea pig, and a snake.

5 Tell students to imagine that the example above is from a piece of student writing titled "Ivan's Zoo" that you received early in the school year. Demonstrate for students how you would edit this sentence during your regular checking (a process we refer to as the Teacher Edit). On the chalkboard, within the margin, add the word *colon* with a circle around it.

6 Distribute a Decoder List to each student and instruct everyone to find the code for *colon*. Use your overhead transparency to help students locate this rule. Have a volunteer read the rule out loud. Make the correction on the sentence on the board, replacing the first comma with a colon before the list of pets, as shown below.

(: colon)   Ivan had six pets: an iguana, two dogs, a parrot, a guinea pig, and a snake.

Distribute a copy of the Personal Skills Record to each student. Instruct students to write their name on the top in the space provided. Tell them to pretend that they wrote the sentence above as part of a story. Now they must copy into their skills record the targeted skills resulting from the teacher's edit. Have each student do this, following directions on the form to record the date and title of the composition, the skill code, and the skill description. Tell them they do not have to copy anything in parentheses or in italics. As they look for the appropriate skill code and description, they will be diving right in to the Decoder List and putting it to immediate use.

Next, display the transparency of the Skills Record Student Sample on the overhead so that students can check their work. Cover the next entry (*a lot/allot*) with a sheet of paper so that only the *colon* entry is visible.

Now have them practice a second entry with a spelling mistake. Write the following sentence on the board, along with the indicated correction code in the margin:

(a lot/allot)   Although he has allot of animals, Ivan wants a ferret for his birthday.

Tell students to pretend that, as in the first example, they wrote this sentence and made this mistake. Have them find the code in the Decoder List—it's in the section labeled Common Spelling Errors (Homonyms)—and copy the skill into their Personal Skills Record. Invite a student to the board to correct the spelling from *allot* to *a lot*.

Instruct students to put the Decoder List and Personal Skills Record in their binders in a section for writing and grammar. Let them know that they will be putting it to frequent use all year long.

Developing Each Student's Personal Skills Record

INTRODUCTION

Once students have copies of the Decoder List and have started their individual Personal Skills Record, they are on their way to developing their own unique forms of grammar goodness—and so are you. The next step is to make sure students develop the regular habit of using these two tools and learning from them.

The most effective and efficient way to begin this process is by assigning writing on a regular basis, collecting it, and doing ungraded Teacher Edits. Becoming familiar with students' most common errors through their writing is the truest way for you to identify the skills and grammar you're going to need to teach. And it's the only way your students can start learning from the rules they are copying and from their own writing. (Note: You can focus on students' spoken language in the same way after they begin to recognize their errors in their written language.)

If you value something, you must give it class time, so make sure you offer students sufficient time to practice revising on their own while using their Personal Skills Record, as well as time to copy the skills from Teacher Edits to the Personal Skills Record.

PURPOSE

What students need to know and be able to do:

◎ Continue adding to their Personal Skills Record

◎ Notice repeated mistakes

And what you'll gain from this lesson:

◎ The start of an ongoing list of grammar and usage lessons that you'll need to teach (based on the most common errors in students' writing)

MATERIALS

◎ Decoder List (included in each student's binder, per Lesson II-1)

◎ Personal Skills Record (in each student's binder, with entries from Lesson II-1)

◎ Recently written, short student compositions, one per student (a book review or the first two pages of a longer piece would work well); these writing pieces should be edited by the teacher, using codes from the Decoder List

Instructional Suggestions

1. Hold a class discussion by inviting students to answer these questions:

    a. Why do teachers correct writing?

    b. How do they make corrections?

    c. Who is really learning from this?

    d. Who is really doing all the work?

    Chances are, the answers you receive will resemble the following:

    a. So they can issue grades

    b. Using codes and abbreviations we don't understand

    c. The teacher

    d. The teacher

2. Tell students that you have decided to give all of this power back to them by putting a moratorium on grades for Teacher Edits for the time being. Remind them of the Decoder List, now part of each student's binder. Tell them that this list will demystify those confusing correction codes. Promise that this will help them to really learn so they will no longer repeat the same writing errors.

3. Distribute to each student his or her own teacher-corrected piece of writing. Allow class time for students to locate the mistakes in their writing, search out the codes on the Decoder List, and copy the skills into their Personal Skills Record. If they do not finish copying all of their skills, assign the balance as homework. Tell students not to discard anything. Alert them that you will check the skills records and writing pieces tomorrow and answer questions.

4. On the next day, collect the skills records and student compositions to check how thoroughly each student has recorded targeted skills. Identify students who need more help in completing this task.

5. Write a short positive comment on each student's Personal Skills Record. Just a few words of encouragement such as "Nicely done" or "Don't worry—I promise we'll have a lesson on run-on sentences next week" make all the difference.

6. Return the Personal Skills Records and the student writing pieces. Instruct students to revise their work, making all corrections on their papers and pursuing any further revisions. Assign a due date for final papers.

7. As the year goes on, you will need to collect the Personal Skills Records less frequently. You will get to the point where you can just circulate around the room and eyeball the records on a regular basis, collecting them only at the end of each term, for a completion grade. However, it is important to check them periodically, or students will just stop working with them.

Teaching Students to Use the Personal Skills Record During Revising
(Before Submitting Work to the Teacher)

INTRODUCTION

When introduced to the step that is the focus of this lesson, students have often commented, "It's almost like cheating! We know what mistakes to catch before the teacher can catch them!" Tell them, "Knock your lights out, kids. Go for it. Catch those mistakes and correct them on your own."

Help students realize that the process is cumulative: Each time they copy a skill into their Personal Skills Record, they are adding to the list of things they'll know to check when they revise the next piece of writing. And remember, now that students have copies of the Decoder List and have started their own Personal Skills Record, they are empowered to develop their own unique forms of grammar goodness—and so are you, because you are compiling a list of frequent errors to address in future lessons.

PURPOSE

What students need to know and be able to do:

- Learn to avoid repeating mistakes by using their own Personal Skills Record during revising—*before* submitting work to the teacher

- Continue adding to their Personal Skills Record

- Notice repeated mistakes

And what you'll gain from this lesson:

- An ongoing list of grammar and usage lessons that you'll need to teach (based on the most common errors in students' writing)

MATERIALS

- Decoder List (included in each student's binder, per Lesson II-1)

- Personal Skills Record (included in each student's binder, per Lesson II-1, with entries from an earlier piece of teacher-corrected writing)

- Student compositions, one per student, not yet submitted for Teacher Edit

Instructional Suggestions

1. Invite students to list the actions they take as they edit and revise their writing before submitting their work to the teacher for a Teacher Edit. Write their comments on the board. Some might include "I read it over and look for mistakes"; "I show it to my parent/babysitter/tutor"; "I ask a friend to correct it"; "I reread old papers"; "I remember my old mistakes"; or, perhaps, "Nothing."

2. Remind them that they now have a tool that will empower them to specifically target problem areas and avoid making the same mistakes without anyone else's help or interference. This is their Personal Skills Record.

3. Instruct students to take out their Personal Skills Record and to read carefully the rules they recorded for the mistakes they made in their last piece of writing. Clarify any questions students might have about these mistakes.

4. Tell students that they will now read through their most recent writing piece to check only for mistakes that they have already recorded on their Personal Skills Record. For example, our sample student, Ophelia Heartbeat, would check her current Personal Skills Record (see page 38) and then read through her new piece to look specifically for a colon before a list; the correct pronoun case; and the spelling of *a lot* and *separate*. With their skills records open and available, students should read their compositions with pencils in hand to note mistakes as they encounter them.

5. Students will probably also pick up other errors as they read, but it's best to have them focus at first on previous errors because they will experience real satisfaction if they can catch themselves repeating an earlier mistake and correct it on their own. Circulate around the room and help students make decisions and corrections.

6. Allow students a second chance to read and revise their work, this time reading their writing out loud, softly, to themselves. You might wish to allow them to spread out on the floor to reduce noise distractions, or even spill into the hallway, if this is practical. The goal in having them read aloud is to allow them to *hear* their own words. This will help them to better discern whether the writing makes sense, to catch new mistakes, and to correct stilted or awkward wording.

7. For homework, have students revise their writing and make the corrections that they have noted. Tell them to reread the final version one more time, out loud, to catch any other mistakes or typos (especially homonym misspellings and missing words), before submitting for Teacher Edit.

8 Close this lesson by asking students to compose a short list of things they now know they can do on their own to edit and revise their writing. Write the list on the board for students to copy. (You might also copy the list to poster paper and display it on a class bulletin board). A sample list follows:

Things I Can Do to Edit and Revise

a. Read my Personal Skills Record and then read my writing with a pencil ready, to catch the same mistakes and correct them.

b. Read my writing out loud, with a pencil ready, and listen for wording and flow.

c. After making all corrections and before submitting, read my writing out loud one more time with a pencil ready, looking especially for typographical errors.

9 Assure students that as the year progresses and they keep updating and using their Personal Skills Record, they will become much more proficient in revising and editing their own papers. The proof of this will come when they notice that they are being asked to copy fewer and fewer skills after Teacher Edits—a sure sign of their own growth and progress.

10 As the year goes on . . .

a. Frequently remind students that they must copy the skills from the Teacher Edits into their Personal Skills Record *every time* they receive teacher-edited copies.

b. Keep your own running list of skills that need attention. These will be based on the most common repeated errors that you note and/or that appear in students' Personal Skills Records. Plan and schedule class lessons for the most frequent problems.

c. Remember to write a short comment each time you review a student's Personal Skills Record, such as "Good progress—fewer skills errors since September!" or "Come for extra help and a grammar snack this week so you won't have to copy the comma splice rule so often." These comments mean a great deal to students—sometimes they are the only good things they have heard about their grammar.

Descriptions of Skills to Copy and Learn

DIRECTIONS: After you receive a writing piece that has been edited and corrected by your teacher, look over the corrections and explanatory codes in the margins. For each code, locate the skill described below and copy both the code and the skill description into your Personal Skills Record (in the writing section of your binder). Remember to use your Personal Skills Record to revise and edit your next piece so that you do not repeat the same mistakes.

CODE	DESCRIPTION OF SKILL TO COPY
1. agr (means "agreement")	Be sure the subject agrees with the verb as singular or plural. *The boy goes; the girls go.* Be sure that a pronoun agrees with the noun it refers to as singular or plural. *The child was happy; he was smiling. The children were angry; they were shouting.*
2. anachronism	This is a word, phrase, thing, or idea that is out of place in time. *John Hancock e-mailed his friends after he signed the Declaration of Independence.*
3. ' apostrophe	Use an apostrophe to show possession. Watch the placement of the apostrophe to show whether the owner is singular or plural: *boy's bike* (belongs to one boy); *boys' room* (belongs to boys).
4. awk (means "awkward")	Read writing out loud and listen for awkward or confusing wording. Revise to clarify for your reader.
5. blend	Blend quotations and direct statements from other writers you reference for a smooth flow of ideas. Do this by using quotation marks around their words while weaving them into your words.
6. cap	Capitalize the first letter of an official title for a person or entity, a word that is used in place of a name in direct address, and any proper nouns. (Capitalize *Mom* when the speaker is directly addressing her—e.g., *Hi, Mom!*; no caps when the speaker is referring to her—e.g., *my mom*; and always capitalize proper nouns like *New York* and *Ms. Merletto*.)
7. cite	Use quotes around words that are not yours. Cite words and ideas that come from another source by putting the author, title, and page number in parentheses in the text of your writing, and in a bibliography as well.
8. ? clarify	Writing may not be clear to the reader; work on clarifying and saying exactly what the reader needs to understand.

9. : colon—letter	Use a colon after the salutation of a business or formal letter. *Dear Sir or Madam:*
10. : colon—list	Use a colon before a list. *Here's what we need:*
11. , comma—appos	Use a comma—or two, as applicable—to set off an appositive. *Ivan, my little brother, put the frog in my sister's backpack.* (An appositive is a noun or a noun phrase that renames a noun or a pronoun.)
12. , comma—conj	Use a comma before conjunctions (such as *and, but, or, nor, yet*) when the conjunctions connect complete clauses in a compound sentence. *The punishment for Ivan was to clean Ophelia's fish tank, and Ophelia had to help Ivan return the frog to the garden without screaming.*
13. , comma—dir addrs	Use a comma to set off words of direct address. *Ophelia, stop licking the cream off that Oreo cookie.*
14. , comma—intro	Use a comma to set off long introductory phrases and clauses. *As soon as Ophelia saw that frog gazing up at her, she let out a terrified scream.*
15. , comma—letter	Use a comma after the salutation in a friendly letter. *Dear Electra,* Also use a comma after the closing in all letters. *Sincerely, Ophelia Heartbeat*
16. , comma—nonrestrict	Use a comma to set off nonrestrictive clauses and phrases from the rest of the sentence. (A nonrestrictive clause or phrase relays information that is not essential to understanding the sentence or story.) *My mother, who had lots of brothers, insisted that my sister stop screaming about a frog in her backpack.*
17. , comma—paren exp	Use a comma to set off a parenthetical expression. *My sister's reaction, of course, was over the top.*
18. , comma—quote	Use a comma to set off a direct quote and parts of a divided quote. *"I can't believe that someone," our mother growled, "put that poor frog in Ophelia's backpack."* (If the direct quote ends in a question mark or exclamation point, you don't need a comma. *"Who put that poor frog in Ophelia's backpack?" our mother growled.*)
19. , comma—reread	Read the writing out loud and listen for a soft pause to insert a comma. Be careful not to overuse commas. (Use available workbook practice pages to learn comma rules.)
20. , comma—series	Use a comma to separate words in a series of three or more. *They wrote stories, poems, and jokes.*

21. comma splice	Use a semicolon or a conjunction, NEVER a comma, between two independent clauses when the two clauses are closely related. *They went swimming on Monday; they went boating on Tuesday.* Use a period between two complete sentences, NEVER a comma. *They went swimming on Monday. They played chess all night.*
22. conj (means "conjunction")	In general, avoid using a conjunction to start a sentence; conjunctions tend to be overused. When a conjunction *is* used to start a sentence, it sometimes needs a comma after it to cue the reader. *Yet, Ivan could not resist repeating his trick when he found a cute garter snake the following week.*
23. ~~contraction~~	Do not use contractions in formal writing.
24. – dash	Use the dash to show an emphasis in meaning, or to set off an aside or an explanation. Use one dash this way: *Clementine decided against wearing purple eye shadow to the interview—a wise choice.* Use two dashes this way: *Ivan's dazzling smile—boosted by his daily use of whitening strips—won every girl's heart.*
25. . . . **ellipsis**	Use an ellipsis to show words or lines left out of a quotation. "I pledge allegiance to the flag . . . and to the republic . . ."
26. extended quote	When a quotation from a text is two lines or more, indent the passage in both margins and do not use quotation marks. Include the author's last name and page number at the end of the quotation.
27. few/less	Use *few* if you can count them. Use *less* if you cannot count them. *Express Checkout: 15 Items or <u>Fewer</u>.* (You can count items.) *We brought <u>less</u> soda and <u>fewer</u> bags of chips for the sleepover since Alberta always has plenty at her house.* (You can count bags but you can't count soda.) *The <u>fewer</u> cans of soda that we bring on the hike, the <u>less</u> stuff we'll have to carry.* (You can count cans but you can't count stuff.)
28. format	Use correct format when writing a letter or book review. (Use models for correct format; if you do not have formatted models, check with teacher for correct format.)
29. frag (means "fragment")	Incorporate a sentence fragment into an existing sentence, or turn the fragment into a complete sentence (add the missing noun and/or verb). *Walking down the street and whistling. Walking down the street and whistling, the boy seemed happy.*

30. ~~is when/is where~~   Never use the phrases *is when* or *is where*; substitute with phrases such as *occurs when/where* or *can be seen when.*

31. italics—foreign language   Use *italics,* or <u>underlining</u>, for words in a language other than English, such as Latin or French or Spanish. ("*Buenos dias,*" said the Spanish teacher.)

32. italics—word or sound   Use *italics,* or <u>underlining</u>, for a word in a sentence that represents an example of a sound or word. (*Do,* a deer, a female deer . . .; The word *blue* has one syllable.)

33. ~~I think/I believe~~   In expository or persuasive pieces, avoid writing *I think . . .* or *I believe . . .*; it weakens the argument. Just state your opinion and explain the supporting reasons.

34. lie/lay   The verb *lie* means "to recline." *I lie on the sofa.* (present tense) *I lay on the sofa.* (past tense) It is never followed by a direct object.
The verb *lay* means "to set" or "to place." *I lay the book on the table.* (present tense) *I laid the book on the table.* (past tense) It is always followed by a direct object.

35. model   Use the model provided in class for format, ideas, and content (such as letter format).

36. num (means "number")   Write out numbers of ten and under as words (*8* should be *eight* but *163* should be *163*, not *one hundred and sixty-three*). Write out any number that starts a sentence.

37. ~~of~~   Do not use *of* as a helping verb; it can only be used as a preposition. *I should have, we could have, they would have,* but never *I should of.*

38. P (means "punctuation") —quotations   Put correct punctuation—*!* or *?* or *,*—between a quotation and the phrase that refers to the speaker (*he said*). Never use a period. Use lowercase to start the *he said* phrase after a quotation. *"I'm going out now!" he said.* Start a new paragraph with each new speaker.

39. para (means "paragraphing")   Are there enough paragraphs? Too many paragraphs? Insert new paragraph breaks in the places a reader will need them—for example, when the topic shifts or one speaker stops talking and another begins.

40. ⊙ period   Use a single period as end punctuation. Listen for the natural spot where your voice stops and drops in a sentence.

41. play   When discussing a play, do not call it a "book"; use "play" or "drama" or "script."

42. pronoun case   The object of a preposition always takes objective case. *I gave it to <u>him</u>. To <u>whom</u> are you referring?* Keep this

34

between you and <u>me</u>. The verb *to be* always takes subjective case. *I am <u>she</u>. It was <u>he</u>.*

43. proof	Proofread before submitting for Teacher Edit, especially for missing words, homonym misspellings, sentence structure, and logical development. Refer to your Personal Skills Record and Common Spelling Errors (Homonyms) list.
44. " / " quotation marks	Use quotation marks before and after words said out loud or words written by someone else. (It is your responsibility to check to make sure you acknowledge someone else's words or ideas as theirs and not your own.)
45. ref (means "pronoun reference")	Avoid vague or unclear pronoun reference. *After Ivanna fooled her sister, she fooled her mother.* To whom does *she* refer? Did Ivanna's sister fool her mother, or did Ivanna? You can't tell for sure from the way this sentence is written.Be sure your pronoun agrees in number with the noun to which it belongs (see **agr**).
46. rep (means "repetition")	Listen for the same word or idea repeated in close proximity; substitute another word or phrase (check thesaurus or dictionary).
47. run-on	Read out loud and listen for run-on or convoluted sentences. Condense the sentence or split into two sentences. Hint: If you run out of breath, the sentence is too long! Too many phrases and clauses hooked together with commas and conjunctions can lose a reader and the thread of the idea. (See **comma splice** for correct punctuation.)
48. ; semicolon	Use a semicolon between two independent clauses, NEVER a comma. Use a semicolon to show that the two clauses are closely related. (See **comma splice** for more information.)
49. sent comb (means "sentence combining")	Listen for choppy sentences—many sentences that are too short—and combine them.
50. ' / ' single quote	Use single quotation marks when using a quote within a quote. *He said, "My mother always tells me, 'Wear your boots!'"*
51. ~~slang~~	Do not use slang (such as *kids*) in formal writing.
52. / slash	Use a slash to show a line break in a poem that is being written straight across the page instead of in its usual form.
53. sp (means "spelling")	Add the word to your Personal Skills Record. Revise and proofread before submitting a piece for Teacher Edit. Circle every word you are not absolutely sure of and look it up. Check your Personal Skills Record when proofreading. Do a spell-check before each printing. Watch for words that

are really one word—such as *masterpiece, cannot*—or two words—*a lot, all right*—or homonyms—*their/there; its/it's; weather/whether.* (See list of commonly misspelled homonyms at the end of this Decoder List.)

54. tense	Decide on one tense: past or present. Whenever possible, use present tense when discussing literature or events in literature.
55. than/then	*Than* is used for comparison. *I am taller than you are. Then* is used for time. *We went to math class and then to lunch.*
56. title	Underline or italicize titles of books, plays, movies, magazines, newspapers, or ships. *The Boston Globe* Use quotation marks around short works (poems, short stories, essays, articles). "The Legend of Sleepy Hollow"
57. ~~title~~	Do not underline a title when it is working as a title at the top of your writing piece or manuscript.
58. title and author	Include the title and author in the introduction when discussing a literary work.
59. title caps	Capitalize the initial letter in the first, last, and most important words in a title. Nouns and verbs are usually capitalized; articles and prepositions are not usually capitalized unless first or last in the title. *The Count of Monte Cristo*
60. title content	Brainstorm titles and choose the best words that both invite the reader and fit the piece.
61. went	Do not use *went* with a helping verb (the helping verbs *have, has,* and *had* form the past participle of a verb) because the past participle of the irregular verb *to go* is *gone* (not *went*). Never say *I have went, she has went, they had went,* etc.; instead, say *I have gone, she has gone, they had gone.*
62. wordy	Read your work out loud and listen for too many/too fancy/too complicated words.
63. ~~you~~	Do not use *you* as a generalization. Use *you* only when directly addressing the reader, usually in "how-to" writing. *You* is not usually used in formal expository essays.

COMMON SPELLING ERRORS (HOMONYMS)

| **64.** accept | To agree to something or accept it willingly. *I accept your nomination.* |
| except | Excluding; other than. *Everyone can enter except the dogs.* |

65.	a lot (two words)	Quite a bit, quite a few. *We made a lot of errors in the game.*
	allot (one word)	To parcel out, give in portions. *I will allot one cookie for each child.*
66.	everyday (one word)	Ordinary, regular. *I love everyday people.*
	every day (two words)	Repeated day after day. *We have homework every day.*
67.	hear	To listen to. *I hear you.*
	here	In this place. *Put it here, on the table.*
68.	hole	An empty place. *The boy in Sachar's book has to dig a hole every day.*
	whole	Entire, complete. *The whole test took only 20 minutes.*
69.	its	Shows ownership; belongs to it. *The monster bared its fangs.*
	it's	It is (contraction). *It's scary to see a monster.*
70.	know	To have knowledge. *I know the answer.*
	no	A negative answer. *No, I won't do it.*
71.	principal	The most important, or the head or a school. *The principal thing to learn is to tell the truth. Ms. McNamara is our principal.*
	principle	A rule or belief. *A guiding principle is to tell the truth.*
72.	their	Belonging to them. *They left their hats.*
	there	At that place. *The hats are there on the table.*
	they're	They are (contraction). *They're going to be upset because they lost the best hat.*
73.	to	In the direction of. *We're going to the game.*
	too	Also or very. *That game was too long!*
	two	The number 2. *I've attended two games.*
74.	weather	Sun, snow, rain, and so on. *The weather was beautiful on our vacation.*
	whether	In one case or another. *Whether you like it or not, you must learn these!*
75.	where	In a place. *Where is the game today?*
	wear	To be clothed in. *Will you wear the dress or the skirt?*
76.	whose	Possessive form of *who*. *Whose turn is it?*
	who's	Who is (contraction). *Who's going to the fair tonight?*
77.	your	Possessive form of *you*. *It's your turn next.*
	you're	You are (contraction). *You're the next batter up.*

Personal Skills Record

Name: __Ophelia Heartbeat__

1. Write the date and title of your teacher-edited writing piece.

2. Write the correction code word or symbol indicated in a circle on your teacher-edited piece.

3. Write (and learn!) the entire rule for each skill or homonym spelling identified in a circle on your teacher-edited piece. (Use the Decoder List to find the code and rule.) The first time you break a rule, put a check next to that rule.

4. If the Teacher Edit points out a spelling error for a word that is not on the homonym list, just copy the correctly spelled word that the teacher has written.

5. Refer to your own Personal Skills Record list to help you edit and revise before you hand in each piece of writing.

6. Add to this list each time you receive a Teacher Edit. If you copied the rule for a previous writing piece but made the mistake again on a new one, you must copy the rule again. Note repeats by starring them.

Date	Title	Code word/ symbol	Skill: Use the Decoder List and copy the entire skill rule (except the material in parentheses or in italics).
9/10	"Ivan's Zoo"	: colon—list	✔ Use a colon before a list.
		a lot/allot	✔ a lot Quite a bit, quite a few.
			allot To parcel out, give in portions.
9/21	"Bad Day"	pronoun case	✔ The object of a preposition always
			takes objective case. The verb *to be*
			always takes subjective case.
		: colon—list	* Use a colon before a list.

Personal Skills Record

Name: _____

1. Write the date and title of your teacher-edited writing piece.

2. Write the correction code word or symbol indicated in a circle on your teacher-edited piece.

3. Write (and learn!) the entire rule for each skill or homonym spelling identified in a circle on your teacher-edited piece. (Use the Decoder List to find the code and rule.) The first time you break a rule, put a check next to that rule.

4. If the Teacher Edit points out a spelling error for a word that is not on the homonym list, just copy the correctly spelled word that the teacher has written.

5. Refer to your own Personal Skills Record list to help you edit and revise before you hand in each piece of writing.

6. Add to this list each time you receive a Teacher Edit. If you copied the rule for a previous writing piece but made the mistake again on a new one, you must copy the rule again. Note repeats by starring them.

Date	Title	Code word/ symbol	Skill: Use the Decoder List and copy the entire skill rule (except the material in parentheses or in italics).

PART III

Direct Teaching the Core Knowledge
(Without Carrying a Big Stick)

*Like everything metaphysical,
the harmony between thought and reality
is to be found in the grammar of language.*

—Ludwig Wittgenstein

Do you have some students who use sentence fragments that obscure the meaning of their writing? Do others mess up on pronoun case, saying, "Between you and I" or "He's faster than me"? Do some liberally sprinkle paragraphs with comma splices and run-ons? And when they do these things, do you mark the mistakes, correct them, and teach lessons on these issues? Great!

However, the problem is that during these lessons we find ourselves using what Fine and Josephson call "Grammarspeak" in *More Nitty-Gritty Grammar* (Ten Speed Press, 2001). Because most students do not know the language of grammar, using Grammarspeak propels us all down a slippery slope of confusion and misunderstanding. Thus, when we patiently explain that it should be "between you and me" because the object of the preposition in a prepositional phrase always takes objective case, students' eyes glaze over. Before they can even begin to understand that sentence, they must understand the "foreign-language terms" that it contains: *preposition, phrase, pronoun, objective case*. To understand these concepts, they must also have a working knowledge of the difference between a *noun* and a *pronoun* or a *phrase* and a *clause*. As one thing leads to another, down we go on that slippery slope, losing them again and again because we can't teach it all in one lesson.

You and your students need a break! Stop, take a deep breath, and start thinking of the language of grammar as a foreign language that everyone needs—and deserves—to learn. Call it, if you like, by this new name—Grammarspeak. Explain to your students that we all need to understand this foreign language in order to communicate about how to improve our writing and our speaking, as well as to talk intelligently about what we appreciate in others' uses of language. Then, teach them this new language by using the techniques of foreign-language teachers: basic and patient explanations of even the most simple vocabulary words, oral recitation and repetition, memorization, and opportunities to practice application. Part III provides two introductory lessons to help you do just that, and then follows up with five lessons that elaborate on specific Grammarspeak essentials.

Learning the Language of Grammar: Parts of Speech

INTRODUCTION

We admit this is not usually a topic that makes a student's heart sing; but let's face it, the parts of speech are the basic building blocks of our language. Each block has a specific function that helps create meaning in a sentence. So, if our students are going to learn Grammarspeak, we have to give them some basic vocabulary. (Note: If you are certain that your students are secure in their understanding of the parts of speech, you may choose to use this as a review lesson or even to skip this lesson altogether.)

No matter how you use the lesson, it will be helpful to distribute the Definitions: Parts of Speech handout (see pages 47–49) for students to have as a handy reference in their binders.

PURPOSE

What students need to know and be able to do:

⊚ Learn the names of the parts of speech

⊚ Identify and label the parts of speech in a context

⊚ Use the parts of speech purposefully and correctly in writing and speaking

⊚ Understand that words are powerful: They can be weapons of destruction; toys to play around with; tools of persuasive and creative force

MATERIALS

⊚ One photocopy for each student of the Definitions: Parts of Speech reproducible (pages 47–49)

⊚ Grammar books

⊚ Dictionaries

Instructional Suggestions

1. Explain the concept of Grammarspeak to students. Tell them that you will be giving them the tools and keys to unlock this foreign language. Explain, too, that there are two basic categories within this language—parts of speech and part of a sentence. This lesson focuses only on the former.

2. Distribute to each student a photocopy of Definitions: Parts of Speech. Instruct students to keep this glossary in the grammar section of their binders.

3. Read over the definitions in class, making sure each student says each term aloud. We recommend having the entire class read the term first, followed by an individual student reading the definition aloud and a second student reading the sample sentence. You then can comment on the additional information about that term.

4. If you follow this same procedure for all the terms, going around the room to make sure all students are called on, you'll guarantee that the students themselves are reading all the information. Resist the temptation to be the one who reads the terms and definitions out loud for the students. They are learning a new language and must get practice in speaking, pronouncing, and hearing these terms and concepts on their own and from one another.

5. Feel free to offer additional information as you work through the list. For example, you might suggest that whenever students are unsure about the part of speech of a word, they can look it up in the dictionary. Give them a word, say, *fandango*, *peregrination*, or *troglodyte* (or any word they're not likely to know), and have them find the word in their dictionary. Help them discover that the part of speech is abbreviated in italics, followed by a pronunciation guide, a definition, and, typically, at least one synonym. Point out, too, that the dictionary entry includes, when applicable, ways the word can be changed to become another part of speech and therefore used in a different way in a sentence. Depending on the dictionaries you are using, you might want to add that the etymology of the word is also provided.

6. Be forewarned that there are hidden complexities within most parts of speech. Questions will inevitably arise. For instance, **nouns** seem straightforward enough: They name something. But students may wonder why some words can be both nouns and verbs (for example, *run, report, fly, fire, wire*). You can explain that, in fact, it's part of our English language tradition to "verb" our nouns and "noun" our verbs. Here's your opportunity to explain the unique magic of the English language: By changing the position of a word in a sentence and/or adding another ending to the word, we can transform many nouns into verbs; verbs into nouns; and adjectives into adverbs. For example, in the sentence, *"Ready, set, fire," ordered the captain*, *fire* is a verb. It

describes an action. But in this sentence, *Clementine built a fire in the old woodstove, fire* is a noun, a thing. One pass through this will not be sufficient, so promise your students that you'll explain more about this when you consider verbs.

7 **Pronouns** are hard to learn and tough to teach because they are inflected—that is, they have case, number, and gender, and each one requires an antecedent. Besides all that there are several categories of pronouns:

- ◉ **Personal pronouns:** the three subcategories are subject pronouns (nominative case); object pronouns (objective case); and ownership pronouns (possessive case).

- ◉ **"Mirror" or reflective pronouns:** e.g., *myself, yourself, himself, themselves.*

- ◉ **Relative pronouns:** *who, whom, whose, that,* and *which.*

- ◉ **"Pointing" or demonstrative pronouns:** *that, these, this, those.*

- ◉ **"Question" or interrogative pronouns:** *which, what, who, whom, whose* (notice that some of these pronouns have more than one role to play).

- ◉ **Indefinite pronouns:** e.g., *all, anybody, someone.*

With all these categories of pronouns, each with its own rule for use, it's no wonder students get confused. And it's no surprise that we have to undertake a considerable amount of direct instruction to teach pronouns—but *please*, not all at once. Spread it out and plan on lots of recursive teaching and learning. There's much for students to take in. Patient explanation, repetition, memorization, and opportunities to practice are the way we learn any language, including Grammarspeak. (And to help your students gain some of that needed experience, you can use Practice for Pronoun Power!, pages 111–113 in the Appendices.)

8 Now is a good time to stop and take one of those deep breaths. Tell your students they don't have to absorb all of this information on nouns and pronouns, or any other parts of speech, all at once. Remind them that they and you have excellent grammar books to serve as references. (See the list of recommended student-friendly grammar books in Part I, page 16, as well as the Bibliography.) Assure them that together you and they will work to grow their knowledge of Grammarspeak and their powers of grammar goodness.

9 When your students are reviewing **verbs,** remind them about the many words in English that can be nouns as well as verbs, depending on their use in a sentence (see step 6). Once students understand that verbs describe an action (or state of being) and tell time, they can easily identify them in a sentence. You may want to say something about verbals (gerunds, present

participles, past participles, and infinitives). We address verbals in the Parts of the Sentence lesson (page 50). For now, if you choose to say anything about them, you might explain that by adding –*ing* or –*ed* to a verb, you can use that verb as a noun or an adjective. For example:

<u>Diving</u> is an Olympic sport. In this sentence, *diving* is used as a noun.

or

<u>Diving</u> in icy water, Andre got a cramp. Here, *diving* is an adjective modifying *Andre*.

or

His <u>cramped</u> leg kept him from <u>competing</u>. In this sentence, *cramped* is an adjective and *competing* is a noun.

or

He has learned <u>to dive</u> in warmer water. Here the infinitive *to dive* is a noun.

This kind of flexibility is what makes English such a dynamic language. (When the need arises, you can address the perfect tenses. Your grammar reference books will help your students understand the present perfect, past perfect, and future perfect.)

10 Generally, students are comfortable with **adjectives** because they sprinkle their everyday speech with so many of them, even if they don't know they are using something called "adjectives." But the adjectives most likely to confuse them are the *absolutes*, words such as *unique, final, perfect, dead,* and so on. The list is long. You will need to explain that there is no comparative or superlative for this kind of adjective. You can't be deader, or more final, or more unique, or more perfect than anyone or anything else.

11 As teachers, we are sometimes tempted to tell students that they can recognize **adverbs** because they end in –*ly*. That's true for some adverbs, but it's also true for some adjectives—e.g., *lovely* and *lonely*. Tell students that when in doubt, they should check the dictionary. Adverbs can cause other problems for students because in addition to modifying verbs, they can also modify adjectives and other adverbs, such as:

Cleo felt <u>a little</u> hungry. Here, *little* is an adverb modifying the adjective *hungry*, which is how Cleo felt.

Cleo ate <u>a little</u> dinner. In this sentence, *little* is an adjective modifying the noun *dinner*, which is the kind of dinner Cleo ate.

12 Review with students that a **preposition** is a word that shows how a noun or pronoun is related to another noun or pronoun in a sentence in terms of place, direction, or time. Tell students that in order to remember a good list of prepositions, all they need to do is to learn the "Preposition Song" (see page 19)! They will then know most of the prepositions in our language and be able to figure out the rest when they encounter them. You might also point out that in the "Preposition Song," different prepositions show how the noun *monkey* can relate to the noun *weasel*: *around* the mulberry bush, *in* fun. Some students like to learn that prepositions tell how an angel can relate to a cloud while flying: *on* the cloud, *under* the cloud, *from* the cloud, *through* the cloud, *after* the cloud.

13 **Conjunctions** seem simple, but they can get complicated if students analyze sentences carefully. For most classroom purposes, your students need only focus on the coordinating conjunctions (*and, or, but, for, nor, so, yet*). For a closer study of conjunctions, including the correlative group (*either/or, not only/but also*, etc.) and the subordinating group (*because, unless, since*, etc.), turn to your trusty grammar reference book(s).

14 **Interjections** are words we love to use and sprinkle liberally in our speech and informal writing. Examples include *Hooray! Yay! Rats! Goodness! Awesome!* Interjections are always followed by an exclamation point.

Grammar Lessons You'll Love to Teach   Scholastic Teaching Resources

Definitions: Parts of Speech

1. Nouns are names—of people, places, things, or ideas.

> <u>Athena</u> sprinted down the <u>track</u> to win the <u>race</u> and enjoy her <u>victory</u>.
> *person*   *place*   *thing*   *idea*

Be careful in deciding whether a word is a noun because lots of words in English can be either nouns or verbs, depending on how they're used. Keep this in mind:

- If a word is a noun, it can be made plural (e.g., *victories, races, tracks*).

- If you're still not sure whether a word is a noun, put *the* or *a* or *an* in front of it and see if that makes sense (e.g., *the people, a thing, an idea*).

2. Pronouns (*pro*: "for"; *noun*: "name") are stand-ins for nouns; they take the place of nouns.

> When Achilles was struck in the foot, <u>he</u> knew <u>his</u> fate was sealed.
> *personal pronoun*   *possessive pronoun*

There are several key points to remember about pronouns. Each one has:

- **case**, which means it has a special function in a sentence

- **number**, which means it can be singular or plural

- **gender**, which tells whether it refers to a male or a female or is neutral

- an **antecedent**, which is the noun the pronoun stands in for.

3. Verbs show action or express a state of being at a certain time.

> Manfred <u>fled</u> into the woods, but he <u>was</u> afraid when the wild dogs <u>followed</u> him.
> *action*   *state of being*   *action*

- If a word is a verb, it has tense, i.e., it tells time. The action or the state of being can be in present tense (today), past tense (yesterday), or future tense (tomorrow).

> This year Mario <u>plays</u> soccer. Last year he <u>played</u> beach volleyball.
> *present time*   *past time*

> Next year I predict he <u>will play</u> something else.
> *future time*

- State-of-being verbs work the same way:

am, is, are	indicate present tense
was, were	indicate past tense
will be	indicates future tense.

- Caution: Don't be confused by words such as *now* or *then* or *later*. They are not verbs because you can't change time with them: *now* is always now; *then* is then; *later* is later.

4. Adjectives describe or modify nouns. They tell what kind, how many, or which one.

> Pandora wondered what was in her <u>small</u> box.
> *what kind*

 ⑥ Adjectives can show comparisons—e.g., *small, smaller, smallest* and
    good, better, best.

 ⑥ Some adjectives show comparisons by combining with adverbs (see
    number 5, below), usually the adverbs *more* or *most*, as in:

You are *more talented* at basketball than I am, and Mr. Jackson is the *most talented*
coach I know.

 ⑥ *a, an,* and *the* are adjectives that introduce or signal a noun. They are
    often referred to as **articles**.

> He plays <u>the</u> violin.
> *article*

5. Adverbs describe or modify verbs; they can also modify an adjective or even another
adverb. They tell *when, where, why, how,* or *to what extent.*

> <u>Very cautiously</u>, Chester stepped onto the frozen lake.
> *to   how*
> *what*
> *extent*

> He had to get across <u>soon</u> because the ice was melting.
> *when*

 ⑥ Many adverbs are made by adding *–ly* to certain adjectives, e.g.,
    generous: generously and *nice: nicely.*

 ⑥ Adverbs, like some adjectives, can show degrees of comparison, e.g., *far,
    farther, farthest.* Sometimes they show comparison by including the
    modifying adverbs *more* or *most: kindly, more kindly, most kindly.*

6. Prepositions show relationships between objects and ideas. They indicate position or time,
and they also compare and connect.

> Jake discovered a pot <u>of</u> gold <u>in</u> his backyard.
> *connect   position*

> Most students agreed that the race <u>for</u> class president
> *connect*

was only <u>between</u> Lester and Sarah. Tanya voted <u>for</u>
> *compare*   *connect*

Pandora. Surprisingly, the votes were evenly divided <u>among</u> the three candidates.
> *compare*

 ⑥ Prepositions are followed by nouns (noun phrases and noun clauses) or
    object pronouns (*me, him/her, them/us*).

 ⑥ Don't get hung up on the rule of never ending a sentence with a
    preposition. Experts now agree that that's sometimes the best way to
    make your point.

7. Conjunctions connect words to words and one part of a sentence to another.

> Dumb <u>and</u> Dumber deserve each other.
> *word to word*

> Barney couldn't leave the lighthouse <u>until</u> the fog lifted.
> *one part of sentence to another*

The most obvious conjunctions are *and, or, but, nor, so, yet,* and *for.* Yes, we know, *for* is also a preposition and so is *until,* but they can also function as conjunctions. In the sentence above, *until* is connecting the first part of the sentence to the second part.

8. Interjections are words we love to use because they show feelings. Usually, they are at the beginnings of sentences.

> <u>Good grief</u>! Charlie Brown missed the ball again!
> *interj*

> <u>Oh</u>! What else did you expect?
> *interj*

> <u>Hey</u>! Let's try to cheer up good ole Charlie Brown.
> *interj*

> ☺ Curse words are interjections, but we don't advise using them.

> ☺ The good news is that there are no rules for using interjections. Awesome!

Learning the Language of Grammar: Parts of the Sentence

INTRODUCTION

Many students have no idea why or how there is a difference between parts of speech and parts of a sentence. Thus, a key starting point for this lesson is to help students understand that there are two different basic categories in Grammarspeak—the one they've already learned (parts of speech) and the one they'll learn in this lesson (parts of the sentence).

Learning to label sentences teaches students about both categories in the context of writing. More important, it gives them the power to discuss sentence structure in a common language that is precise and accurate—the language of grammar. Once they are able to identify the different parts of a sentence, they can then be more accurate in identifying which part of speech applies to a particular word, since parts of speech depend on how the word is being used in a sentence.

To some, labeling sentences is reminiscent of diagramming sentences, but there are important differences. Labeling is done right on the sentence, not separate from it, and not on a diagram. There is no need for a ruler or graph paper or answer sheet. When you diagram a sentence, you take it apart; when you label a sentence, you show and identify its parts.

In labeling a sentence, students write the parts of the sentence above the sentence and the parts of speech below the sentence. This helps students see right away how both categories are different and yet closely related. The pattern of the sentence emerges as soon as the sentence is labeled; thus, students gain immediate knowledge about the sentence that they can use to improve or develop their writing.

PURPOSE

What students need to know and be able to do:

⑥ Learn the names of the parts of the sentence

⑥ Identify and label the parts of a sentence and parts of speech

⑥ Use knowledge of the parts of a sentence to make correct choices in key grammar issues: pronoun case, punctuation, and sentence fragments

- One photocopy for each student of Definitions: Parts of the Sentence (pages 54–55)

- Transparency of Definitions: Parts of the Sentence

- One photocopy for each student of the practice activity sheet pages (see Appendices, pages 114–119)

- Transparencies of the same practice sheets

- Grammar books and workbooks, for additional or alternative practice exercises

- Current newspapers

- Popular magazines

Instructional Suggestions

1 Explain to students that the parts of a sentence are one category of Grammarspeak; the parts of speech—which they've already studied—are a completely separate category.

2 Distribute to each student a photocopy of Definitions: Parts of the Sentence. Instruct students to keep this glossary in the grammar section of their binders, directly following the Definitions: Parts of Speech sheet from the previous lesson.

3 Read over the definitions in class, making sure each student says each term aloud. We recommend having the entire class read the term first, followed by an individual student's reading the definition aloud. You then can comment on the additional information about that term.

4 If you follow this same procedure for all the terms, going around the room to make sure all students are called on, you'll guarantee that the students themselves are reading all the information. Resist the temptation to be the one who reads the terms and definitions out loud for the students. They are learning a new language and must get practice in speaking, pronouncing, and hearing these terms and concepts on their own and from one another.

5 Help students understand that the parts of a sentence contain the parts of speech, but also that the parts of speech depend on what function they are playing as parts of the sentence. In fact, a student may query again (see step 6 in the previous lesson): "What about nouns and verbs?" This will be your chance to remind students that they will only be able to identify whether certain words are nouns or verbs (remember our examples, *run*, *report*, *fly*, *fire, wire*) depending upon how they are used in a sentence. Explain or explain again (this kind of repetition never hurts!) that if *fly* is the subject of a sentence (or a direct object, an indirect object, or the object of a preposition in a prepositional phrase), it is a noun. However, it can be a verb if it is used as the predicate in a sentence. Here are two more example sentences:

Noun/subject of the sentence: *The fly landed on my nose.*

Verb/predicate of the sentence: *Harry will fly on his new broom in the match.*

6. Distribute to each student a photocopy of the activity sheet, Practice 1: Label Parts of the Sentence (see Appendices, pages 114–115) and display a transparency of this same activity sheet on the overhead projector. Note: If your students are already fluent in these topics, you might want to jump ahead to Practice 3 (Appendices, pages 118–119). However, we feel that reviewing these terms quickly is a good idea; it builds confidence and fluency for the more difficult sentence work to come.

Follow this procedure to present the practice page:

a. Read aloud the steps, as well as the sample sentence.

b. Be sure to go through the definitions of the parts of a sentence in the order they're presented on the sheet. Using the transparency, label the first sentence with the class.

c. As you label each part of the sentence, explain the label in a complete sentence that includes the definition of the term. Tell students that you are modeling for them what they will be doing in this activity. Example: "The predicate of this sentence is *threw* because it is a verb that shows action or being."

d. Pair each student with a partner. Instruct pairs to label the next three sentences, following the steps in order and defining each label in a complete sentence.

e. Go over these three sentences with the class, calling on volunteers (or, alternatively, going around the room in seat order, allowing students who are unsure to "pass"). Resolve questions and issues as they come up.

f. Each time a student gives an answer, require him or her to announce it in a complete sentence, using the definition page. (See the example in step c above.) This is a crucial part of students' learning this new language of grammar.

g. Instruct students to label the remaining sentences on their own.

h. When students have finished, place the answer key on the overhead, and review each sentence, answering questions as they arise.

i. Assign homework that involves labeling additional sentences. Remind students to use the steps in order.

j. In class the next day, put a homework answer key on the overhead and ask which sentences were problematic. Go over those issues.

7 Use this procedure for other practice sheets involving sentence labeling (Appendices, pages 120–123, and others that you create based on these models). As you go around the room, having students say aloud their sentence labels and explanations, you might think that the exercise is repetitive and formulaic. Of course it is. However, it is also helping your students to do what they do when learning a foreign language: They are having the opportunity to practice speaking and thinking the language of grammar. It is very satisfying when, at the end of class, you can let them all applaud themselves for speaking a new language in complete sentences in only one day!

8 To create your own practice pages, consider using the following kinds of material for sentence labeling:

a. With the student's permission, select an exemplary sentence (preferably one that is funny or outrageous) from a piece of student writing.

b. Choose high-interest articles from newspapers (when screened ahead, certain tabloid articles can provide a great source of material for this activity) or magazines selected by the students.

c. Choose sentences from the literature being studied in class for this activity.

Definitions: Parts of the Sentence

1. The **predicate** shows action (*swooped, screamed, twitters*) or a state of being (the verb *to be* in any of its magical forms: *is, am, are, was, were*). It includes the main verb and any helping verbs (*leaps/is leaping; snarled/had snarled*) along with any modifiers that describe the main verb and helping verbs.

> *pred.*   *pred.*
> The bird <u>screamed</u>. The lion <u>had snarled</u> at it.

2. The **subject** is the main noun or a pronoun and any modifiers that describe the main noun or pronoun. The predicate tells what the subject does or is. To find the subject, ask *who* or *what* before the verb.

> *subj.*
> <u>Louisa</u> read that book all day long.

3. The **object** completes the predicate.

> ◎ To find the **direct object**, ask *whom, who,* or *what* after the predicate.
>
> > *dir. obj.*
> > Igor dropped his <u>backpack</u> on the chair.
>
> ◎ The **indirect object** tells to whom or to what the action of the predicate was done. To find the indirect object, ask *to whom* or *to what* after the predicate.
>
> > *indir. obj.*
> > Luca gave the <u>cat</u> a special treat.
>
> ◎ The **subject complement** completes the linking verb predicate. Linking verbs are the verb *to be* and verbs of the senses, such as *smell, sound, taste, feel, look, seem, appear, become.*
>
> > *subj. comp.*
> > Tasha looked <u>happy</u> at her birthday party.

4. A **phrase** is a group of words without a subject or a predicate. There are several kinds of phrases, including:

> ◎ **prepositional phrases**, which always begin with a preposition: *to the store; from school*
>
> ◎ **participial phrases**, which always begin with a participle (verb + *–ing* or verb + *–ed*): *walking backward; unconcerned with*
>
> ◎ **infinitive phrases**, which always begin with an infinitive (*to* + a verb): *to go; to care.*

5. A **clause** is a group of words with a subject and a predicate. Clauses can function as subjects, objects, adjectives, or adverbs. There are both:

      ⓘ **independent clauses,** which stand alone as complete sentences:

      indep. clause   *indep. clause*
      <u>The lion snarled</u> and <u>the bird screeched</u>.

      ⓘ **dependent clauses,** which must be attached to an independent clause:

      indep. clause   *dep. clause*
      <u>The bird screeched</u> <u>because the lion snarled</u>.

Note to the teacher: These definitions are meant to be simple reminders to students as to the definitions of the basic parts of the sentence. Refer your students to their grammar books for more detailed definitions and explanations of the use in sentences. (See the Bibliography list of recommended student-friendly grammar books.)

Putting Grammarspeak to Work: Verbs Rule! (Imperatively)

INTRODUCTION

Verbs are the most important part of speech in the English language. Without a verb, there is no sentence. It's that simple. One verb can be a complete sentence. Think about it; you see and hear verbs as complete sentences every day.

STOP!   RUN!   GO.
YIELD!   THROW.

Verbs describe action or a state of being at a certain time. There are several easy ways to recognize a verb. Perhaps the easiest is that a verb tells time—that is, it has tense. In each of the verbs listed above, the time is understood to be now, the present tense. Verbs must also agree with the subject of the action or state of being. The subject for the verbs in the list above is "you," which is understood. Another hallmark of verbs is that they make statements in different ways (called "moods"). The two moods that are most common are the indicative (all of the sentences in this paragraph are in the indicative mood) and the imperative (all the verbs in the list above are in the imperative mood). Indicative verbs tell or indicate; imperative verbs give commands.

Sounds simple; unfortunately, our students don't always understand what seems obvious to us. And they are often thoroughly confused by the concepts of tense and mood. In order for students to begin to take control of their language, they have to recognize verbs when they read them and have a solid understanding of how to use and manipulate this wonderfully flexible part of speech.

In this lesson, as in all others in this book, we believe that you can best help your students learn to use language correctly by providing an appropriate degree of direct teaching and immediately following this with active, real-life application. Thus, steps 1 through 3 describe direct instruction; steps 4 through 7 offer an applied activity.

PURPOSE

What students need to know and be able to do:

- ⑥ Recognize verbs in context
- ⑥ Control verb tense in their writing
- ⑥ Understand the different forms (tense, number, mood, and so on) of verbs

MATERIALS

⊚ Transparency of model Recipe Poem (see page 58)

⊚ Books of poetry to demonstrate different styles of poems

⊚ Transparency of Definitions: Parts of Speech reproducible, as well as a copy for each student (in their binders)

Instructional Suggestions

1 Use the following procedures for the direct instruction portion of this lesson:

⊚ Review the basic definition of verbs on the Definitions: Parts of Speech reproducible.

⊚ Write the list of verbs from page 56 (STOP, YIELD, GO, RUN, and THROW) on the board. Invite students to examine this list with you. Call on students to determine for each verb the tense (time) and type (action or state of being).

⊚ Explain to students that these verbs are also called *imperatives*— i.e., they are used for giving commands and directions.

⊚ With students, analyze these verbs for subject (the understood "you"—always the subject of an imperative verb).

⊚ Engage students in a discussion about situations in which imperative verbs are called for; that is, when do we need to give commands or directions? Elicit responses such as: in street signs, in sports, in classrooms, in manuals, in cookbooks, in how-to books.

Note that most students will probably know a good deal about the information described above without necessarily recognizing the term *imperative*. Be sure to call on this prior knowledge as you help students build their grammar concepts (in this and all other lessons).

2 Allow students to put their knowledge to immediate use, not only to reinforce their understanding of verbs, but also of other related language conventions and structures. Explain that they will have a chance to write a poem that describes a "recipe" for achieving or accomplishing something. Possible ideas might include How to Plan a Surprise Party, How to Chair a School Government Committee, How to Be an Effective Team Captain or Team Player, or even How to Survive a Family Vacation.

3 Using a transparency, present a model Recipe Poem to the class. Use the poem to point out how it follows a deliberate pattern and how each rule, step, or direction begins with an imperative. See page 58 for a sample Recipe

Poem, with imperatives underscored. (Incidentally, this is only one possible framework—you and your students can let your imaginations run free for future Recipe Poem patterns.)

How to Survive a Family Vacation

<u>Accept</u> it—you are going to
Lake Winnipesaukee with your
       dad
       mom and
       little brother
For three weeks.

<u>Charge</u> your cell phone.
<u>Stay</u> in touch with
       Leroy
       Carmen and
       Orlando
Every day you're away.

<u>Pack</u> your jeans, tees, sneaks and
<u>Stash</u> in a backpack your
       iPod
       CD player and
       laptop
To stay connected to the world.

<u>Imagine</u> you are about
To be launched into
       outer space
       an undersea cavern
       the inner sanctum
For scientific purposes.

<u>Return</u> after three weeks,
Happy to be
       redefined
       refreshed and
       reconnected to your
       dad, mom,
And little brother
For . . . ever.

4 Now challenge students to create their own Recipe Poem. Invite each student to think of a personally interesting or intriguing subject that involves the presentation of a set of rules, steps to follow, or directions for doing something.

5 Once students have chosen a topic, challenge them to tease out and brainstorm the key rules, steps, or directions involved in the process they want to describe. You might want to pair students with partners so that they can bounce ideas off each other.

6 Based on the lists they have generated and the model you have provided, students write their original poems.

7 A few final comments: You can see that in creating a Recipe Poem, students have to come up with parallel structures and prepositional phrases and write a complete sentence in each stanza. They are also playing with an invented poetic form and with language. As you know, that's really what grammar is all about.

Putting Grammarspeak to Work: Verbs Rule! (Tensely)

INTRODUCTION

Have you ever wondered, after reading a set of student papers, if your students have Chinese as their native tongue, since it's a language without verb tenses? That thought may have crossed your mind because so often in our students' writing there's a meaningless back and forth between past time and present time. These tense shifts not only distract the reader's attention from the student's writing, but they can often interfere with meaning. The truth is that students make these tense errors because they don't understand verb tense forms. That means we have to help them learn what they don't know.

PURPOSE

What students need to know and be able to do:

- ⊚ Recognize verbs in context
- ⊚ Control verb tense in their writing
- ⊚ Understand the different forms (tense, number, mood, and so on) of verbs

MATERIALS

- ⊚ Transparency of the model story "My Appendix" (see page 61)
- ⊚ Transparency of the model story "Speechless!" (see page 61)
- ⊚ Grammar books and workbooks that review verb tenses

Instructional Suggestions

1 Review with students what they already know about verbs. They should understand by now that verbs convey action or a state of being and that they must agree with their subject. From the previous lesson, students should also be aware of the nature of imperatives and should have a basic sense of verb tense.

2 Tell them that in this lesson they'll learn more about verb tense, which is one of the most important forms of any verb. Once they've mastered verb tense, they'll be able to coherently and fluidly tell a story, describe historical events, or refer to a future occurrence.

3 Using a transparency, display the model story below. Read it aloud to the class (or have a volunteer read it aloud). Tell students to focus on both the meaning of the story and on the verb tense (or time) in which the story is written.

My Appendix

One night when I was seven years old, I was awakened by a terrible pain in my stomach. I wanted to cry out for my mother, but I didn't because I didn't want to wake the baby. I didn't want to make my mother angry, so I hid my face in the pillow. But the pain got worse, and finally I crawled out of bed and went to my mother. I was cold, but my body was drenched with sweat. My mother wrapped me in a blanket and called the doctor, who told her to get me to the hospital immediately. By now I was screaming in pain and for good reason because my appendix was about to burst. Later the doctor told my mother that had we delayed a few more minutes, I could have died.

4 As you discuss this story with students, ask if the outcome of the story is ever in question (i.e., is there a chance that the narrator will die?). Students should arrive at the conclusion that it is not. Since the story is told in the first person and is related in past tense, students should realize that—as frightening as the episode was for the storyteller—he or she is still alive, and so it shouldn't generate any genuine fear in readers.

5 Now challenge students to go through the story and change all the verbs to present tense. On the transparency, cross out the past-tense verbs and replace them with students' suggested present-tense equivalents (be sure to correct any suggestions that are incorrect).

6 Read the new version aloud and ask students to decide which version is better for this story. It doesn't really matter which version they prefer, though they are most likely to choose the one in present tense because it winds up sounding more suspenseful. The point of the exercise is to have students focus on verbs, correctly change each from past to present tense, and assess the effect on the story.

7 To reinforce students' learning, share another story with the class. Using a transparency, display the following model story:

Speechless!

I was ten years old and in a one-act Christmas play. I had two lines to say. They were the first two lines in the play: "Well, children, it is almost time for Christmas. What do you want Santa to bring?" That was all I had to say.

The night of the performance I was standing in the middle of Caledonia Elementary School's new stage in a long green-and-white-checked dress my mother had made. I don't remember the curtain rising, just the gymnasium filled with folding chairs. In each of them was a parent staring at me. I blinked as I peered back at them.

Why was I there? I couldn't remember. I heard a familiar voice from way off. I turned my head toward the sound. Miss Budd, my short, chubby fifth-grade teacher, was standing in the wings, the script clutched in her hands. I finally made out her words: "Say your lines!"

Lines, I thought. What lines? I turned back to the audience and opened my mouth. Nothing came out. I could feel my face growing red and hot. I wanted to run, but my feet wouldn't move. Instead I twisted my fingers together and turned imploringly toward Miss Budd.

She understood. She nodded and then called out the first word. "Well," she said, and I said, "Well." Then she said, "children," and I said "children." "It," she said, and I said "it." So it went for the rest of my performance. I repeated each word, one at a time.

Finally, it was over. I ducked behind my classmates at the back of the stage where I thought I would die of embarrassment.

8 Ask students to identify the tense in which this story is written. They should be able to recognize that it, too, is in past tense. Ask them if they think this story would be more appealing if it were written in present tense. You might even try rewriting the first few lines of the story to let them hear how it sounds. Probably your students will agree that this piece makes more sense in past tense because it is simply relating an event that happened in the past. Some might also comment that the short paragraphs and dialogue make it more interesting and get the reader involved in the story regardless of tense. Again, the point is not to suggest that one verb tense is better than another, but that we as writers have the freedom to select the verb tense that works best for the stories we want to tell. That's the power of Grammarspeak!

9 Now your students are ready to work on their own stories. Before they begin, review with them the characteristics of a well-written story, such as the details that help readers feel and see and hear what the writer does. Of course, especially within the context of this lesson, one of the characteristics to review will be control of verb tense.

10 To get them started, you might present them with the same prompt that inspired the two sample stories: "Tell about a time you thought you would die, maybe literally, or from fright, or embarrassment, or of laughter, or happiness, or sorrow, or anticipation, or maybe of something I haven't mentioned."

11 Provide sufficient time for them to write a one- or two-paragraph account of that time they "almost died." Call on volunteers to share their stories.

Grammar Lessons You'll Love to Teach   Scholastic Teaching Resources

Putting Grammarspeak to Work: Preposition Power

INTRODUCTION

By now students should be familiar with the "Preposition Song" (see page 19) and should be able to tell themselves that prepositions "take objective case." So it's time to put 'em to work. Prepositions are powerful modifiers, if you know how to use them.

We like to start with some real writing, in this case, the creation of Preposition Poems. This idea originally came to our attention years ago (Zemelman and Daniels, 1985). Although it was used there for a different purpose, we realized that the form could provide an engaging way to involve students in the deliberate and challenging process of saying something in a poem created almost entirely of prepositional phrases. We hope you'll have as much fun with this lesson as we've had.

PURPOSE

What students need to know and be able to do:

⊚ Recognize the difference between a phrase and a clause

⊚ Create prepositional phrases

⊚ Use objective-case pronouns as objects of prepositions

⊚ Write a poem composed entirely, or almost entirely, of prepositional phrases related to a unifying idea

MATERIALS

⊚ Transparencies of the two model Preposition Poems (see pages 64 and 65)

⊚ Definitions: Parts of Speech reproducible (available to each student in his or her binder)

Instructional Suggestions

1. To get started, pull out your Grammar and Snacks Club song (otherwise known as the "Preposition Song"). This will provide you and the class with instant access to a good long list of prepositions to work with. Sing the song again.

2. Remind students that prepositions always take objective case (e.g., *me*, not *I*). If that concept isn't clear to all your students, and it probably isn't, don't fret; creating prepositional poems is designed to help students use and therefore internalize the concept of objects following prepositions. Review, too, that a prepositional phrase always has an object but not a subject or a verb. Only clauses have subjects and verbs. (Thus, *over the fence* is a prepositional phrase—note no subject or verb—but *as the horses jumped over the fence* is a clause, containing the phrase within it.)

3. Explain to students that in this lesson they are going to write prepositional poems, which should be easy and even fun. Assure them that you will show them how first, of course. In fact, you'll present two model poems, which you'll all discuss, before you expect students to write on their own.

4. On a transparency, display the following sample—or one like it, of your own creation. (Note that here, as in other similar models, underlining is provided for your convenience, to indicate students' answers. The model you display originally should contain no underlining.)

   ### The Secret
   <u>Between Larry and me</u> is a secret
   <u>About you</u>
   <u>On a special day</u>
   <u>In the middle</u>
   <u>Of next week</u>
   <u>At your house</u>
   <u>On Fluffernut Drive</u>.
   <u>Until then</u>, that secret is
   <u>For Larry and me</u> to know . . . and
   <u>For you</u> to find out.

   Ask students to identify the prepositional phrases. Have them underline the phrases.

5. If you wish to go a bit deeper with this lesson, challenge students to find the two clauses that are almost hidden in the poem. Work with them as necessary to identify the linking verb *is* in line 1 and to recognize *a secret* as the subject (the title also helps). The complement for this inverted sentence is the entire list of prepositional phrases. The second clause is in the eighth line and again *is* is the verb/predicate, *secret* is the subject, and the prepositional phrases that follow are the complement.

Grammar Lessons You'll Love to Teach Scholastic Teaching Resources

6 Don't be surprised if at least one student makes the mistake of suggesting that *me* is incorrect in line 1, that the pronoun should be *I*. In fact, this suggestion offers an ideal teaching moment, an opportunity to reinforce the need (and the logic) of providing objects for prepositions, even when the object is a compound, e.g., "Larry and me." This is an interesting and indeed frustrating conundrum. People do not make the mistake of saying, "That muffin is for I" or "Give the flowers to she." But many of those same people mistakenly think it's correct to say, "That muffin is for Stanley and I" or "Give the flowers to Rosetta and I." (Pardon our grammar teacher "Grrrr . . . " here!) What we have to do is not just explain the grammatical rationale for object pronouns after prepositions, but also retrain our students' ears to hear the correctness of object pronouns in compounds following prepositions. And as with any skill, conscious repetition results in automatic performance.

7 Continue the lesson by presenting a transparency of a second model for prepositional poetry. A sample follows:

> **The Quest**
> By following your instincts
> From here to there
> Between now and then
> Into the unknown
> With courage and
> Without doubt of failure
> Away you go
> Across the fields,
> Through the woods,
> Over the mountains
> Until you find
> At the end of your quest
> Under a rainbow—
>   waiting there—
>   A pot of gold.

As with the first model, invite volunteers to underline the prepositional phrases.

8 For this second poem, focus on a different aspect of prepositional phrases with students. Ask them:

     ◉ What is the function of the first eight prepositional phrases? (lines 1–6)

     ◉ What is the function of the three prepositional phrases in lines 8–10?

The goal here is for students to realize that the first eight prepositional phrases are functioning as adjectives, describing *you* (line 7), and that the phrases in lines 8–10 are functioning as adverbs, describing *go* (line 7). Refer students to the Definitions: Parts of Speech reproducible (pages 47–49) to help them recall the nature and role of adjectives and adverbs.

    It's worth pointing out that these model poems have embedded in them at least one complete sentence. We encourage students to do this as well in their own prepositional poems because it helps them to frame a complete idea within each poem.

9. Now that students have analyzed the simple structure of the two models, they should be ready to tackle writing their own prepositional poems. Get them started by asking them to brainstorm ideas, either individually or in pairs, for their poems. To reduce any pressure they might feel, encourage them to choose a commonplace topic, such as surprise parties, goals, favorite foods, or a sport.

10. Once students have written a couple or more of these prepositional poems and you have checked the poems and discussed any confusions, you can be assured that students will know the basics about the preposition: that it always takes an object and that it is a versatile sentence part. You'll still need to do a good deal of reinforcing of the use of object pronouns after prepositions. But you and your students will now be well along the path of prepositional power!

Grammar Lessons You'll Love to Teach Scholastic Teaching Resources

Putting Grammarspeak to Work: Relative Pronouns

INTRODUCTION

Comedians Bud Abbott and Lou Costello of 1940s movie fame created a classic dialogue spoofing, of all things, relative pronouns! In this now legendary comedy sketch, Costello, as the head of a sports department, asks his cohort the names of the baseball players in a game they're watching. Abbott helpfully volunteers the names. The problem is that the players have names like "Who" and "What." So when Costello says, "Well, then, who's on first?" and Abbott answers, "Who!" Costello practically wrings his hands. He goes on to ask who's on second. In exasperation, Abbott says, "Who's on first!" And so it goes as Costello gets increasingly confused.

And so it goes with many of our students as they try to understand correct use of relative pronouns: *who, whom, whose, that,* and *which.* This confusion is no surprise when you consider that pronouns are an anachronistic group of words, throwbacks to the Anglo-Frisian roots of English, when the language was highly inflected. Today, pronouns are the only group of English words that have case, number, and gender and require antecedents to make sense. As if that weren't enough, among the six different categories of pronouns, the relative pronouns are the least understood, therefore the most abused.

Truth to tell, within the evolutionary context of the English language, the usage rules of relative pronouns are in obvious transition. Nevertheless, in the land of grammar goodness, we believe it is our responsibility to teach our students the correct use of relative pronouns so that they can decide to break the rules or not, depending on the context in which they use them. In short, we want students to have control of how they use any part of the language, including relative pronouns.

PURPOSE

What students need to know and be able to do:

- ◉ Understand the particular purpose of each relative pronoun

- ◉ Use relative pronouns correctly

- ◉ Recognize correct and incorrect use of relative pronouns in the media and in speech

◎ Your own collected examples (both correct and incorrect) of relative pronouns in use from print and electronic media

◎ Transparency of Definitions: Parts of Speech reproducible (pages 47–49), as well as a copy for each student (in their binders)

Instructional Suggestions

1 Tell students that in this lesson you'll be focusing on only five words—first, the *who/whom/whose* trio and second, the *that/which* pair. All five words fit into a special category of pronouns called *relative pronouns*.

2 Write *who, whom,* and *whose* on the board or on a transparency. Have students refer to their Definitions: Parts of Speech sheet to review that pronouns have case, number, gender, and require an antecedent. Explain that this is true for relative pronouns too, except it's easier. Here's how you can explain why:

   ◎ *who*
   —is always a subject pronoun
   —can be singular or plural
   —can refer either to females or males

   ◎ *whom*
   —is always an object pronoun
   —can be singular or plural
   —can refer either to females or males

   ◎ *whose*
   —is always a possessive pronoun
   —can be singular or plural
   —can refer either to females or males

Already students should realize that relative pronouns are a lot easier to use than the personal pronouns (*I, me, us, him, her,* and so on) with all their requirements for number and gender.

3 To help students understand how relative pronouns are used in real contexts, write examples on a transparency or the board. Below are sample sentences demonstrating the *who, whom, whose* group in action:

Example sentence: Electra tried to remember *who* had lent her a copy of <u>Great Expectations</u>.
Explanation: *Who* is the subject of *had lent* . . . remember, *who* is always a subject pronoun.

Example sentence: Electra made a mental list of everyone *whom* she had seen that day.
Explanation: *Electra* is the subject of *made*; *she* is the subject of *had seen*; *whom* is the object of *had seen*.

Example sentence: Electra was at a loss as to *whose* book she had borrowed.
Explanation: *Whose* refers to the owner of the book. That's easy to see. You just want to make sure not to confuse *who's*, the contraction for *who is*, and *whose*, the possessive pronoun.

4   Use the sentences in step 3 to help students further analyze the use of *who* and *whom*. Tell them that deciding when to use *who* or *whom* is not a mystery at all; in fact it's actually easy. Here's how they can figure it out:

⊚ First, find the predicate(s) in the sentence.

⊚ Next, find the subject(s) for each predicate.

⊚ Then, apply these two rules:
   A predicate without a subject means the subject pronoun *who* is correct.
   A predicate with a subject means the object pronoun *whom* is correct.

Applying these steps to the example sentences works like this:

⊚ In the first sentence, if you remove *who*, *had lent* would have no subject, so *who* is correct.

⊚ In the second sentence, both predicates *made* and *had seen* have subjects, so *whom* has to be correct.

5   Make available to students your collected examples of relative pronouns in use. (See Materials, page 68.) You might display these on a transparency or distribute photocopies of them. Ask students to determine which uses of relative pronouns are correct and which are not. (Caution: In some informal situations, the use of *who* instead of *whom* may be acceptable, even appropriate. We just want students to recognize what is formally correct and then decide which form to use, depending on the social context.) A few of our own favorites follow. (Note that there are four incorrect examples below, in which *whom* should be substituted for *who*, *who* for *whom*, and *whose* for *who's*, marked for your convenience.)

From a political advertisement (only the name is changed):
"Congressman Flapdoodle is the man who fights for your rights, who cares about your family, who understands your concerns. He is the candidate ~~who~~ you can trust."
"Who here knows ~~who~~ he will vote for?"

From a newspaper story:
"I hope they catch who did it. If I knew who did it, I'd turn him in myself."

From a magazine book review:
"Smith dishes out some harsh criticism to the service chiefs, ~~whom~~ he felt were being parochial and caused problems for front-line command."

From a newsmagazine advertisement:

"I am not an American who confuses politics with patriotism."

From a direct-mail flyer:

"Ask yourself, ~~who's~~ country is this anyway?"

6 Invite students to begin their own collections of *who*, *whom*, and *whose* uses and abuses, along with an analysis of what's formally correct or incorrect. Have students share their examples with the class. Caution: Once they start listening, especially in school, they may assemble quite a list of embarrassing grammatical errors and perpetrators. Remind them of the Grammar and Snacks creed (page 17) and ask them to protect the names of offenders. However, make an exception for yourself—you can take it! It's good for students to realize that we all make grammatical errors occasionally. And it helps to let students know that it's okay to question your grammar use; it's a great way to learn . . . and to teach.

7 The correct use of *that* and *which* should be easy for students to learn. There are two issues students need to understand. First, both of these relative pronouns refer to places and things and not to people. You should be aware that some modern linguists accept *that* to refer to people, but in the land of grammar goodness, we do not. We believe *that* dehumanizes people; in fact, we don't like to use it to refer to animals, either. (One of us, for instance, has a gorgeous orange tiger cat, Oscar, who is definitely a *who*, not a *that*!)

The second point about when to use *that* and *which* causes its share of confusion among speakers and writers, but it is really quite simple: *that* introduces an essential (sometimes called a restrictive) clause; *which* introduces a nonessential (sometimes called a nonrestrictive) clause. For example:

Example sentence: Houses *that* are constructed of sticks blow down in windstorms.
Explanation: The pronoun *that* introduces a clause essential to the understanding of the sentence. If you remove the clause *that are constructed of sticks*, you change the basic meaning of the sentence; not all houses blow down in windstorms.

Example sentence: Brick houses, *which* are common in New England, usually survive stormy weather well.
Explanation: The pronoun *which* introduces a nonessential clause in this sentence. If you remove the clause *which are common in New England*, you don't affect the essential idea of the sentence. Notice that nonessential clauses, those beginning with *which*, are set off by commas.

8 By the end of this lesson, you can tell your students that they are experts on the uses and abuses of relative pronouns. They may also be experts in short supply, so their acquired knowledge is very valuable.

Grammar Lessons You'll Love to Teach Scholastic Teaching Resources

Putting Grammarspeak to Work: Mad Libs Grammatizator for Parts of the Sentence

INTRODUCTION

Like an aspiring basketball player learning about all the moves and shots of the game but never getting out on the court to practice, our students need to do more than just recognize parts of the sentence: predicates, subjects, objects, phrases, and clauses. They need to dribble some subjects and drop-shoot some clauses, place some predicates and lay up some phrases to get in the language game with enough skill to create winning sentence structures.

So grab the verbal ball and get ready for sentence parts practice with the Mad Libs Grammatizator.

PURPOSE

What students need to know and be able to do:

- ⑥ Recognize the parts of the sentence
- ⑥ Use them meaningfully in sentences
- ⑥ Learn how and when to punctuate these structures

MATERIALS

- ⑥ One photocopy for each student of the Grammatizator story "Toon Time," pages 73–75
- ⑥ One photocopy for each student of the "Toon Time": Additional Practice reproducible, pages 76–78
- ⑥ Definitions: Parts of the Sentence sheet, available to students in their binder
- ⑥ Story Starter, page 79 (optional)

Instructional Suggestions

1 Ask students how many are familiar with the word game Mad Libs, which asks players to supply parts of speech without any clear context. Probably most of the class will have some familiarity with this popular game. The results can be funny but are usually silly and always pointless—good for a few laughs maybe. Tell students that you have found a new use for this game format. In this lesson you will have them play a structured game that asks them to supply a part of a sentence within a context.

2 Distribute photocopies of the story "Toon Time," pages 73–75. This story has been divided into sections, each of which is missing some sentence parts. In italics, assorted sentence parts are listed above each section. Tell students that their task is to select the appropriate part for each blank space.

3 Organize students in pairs or groups of three for this task. Encourage them to refer to Definitions: Parts of the Sentence (pages 54–55). As long as the sentence part that students select fits into the specified sentence part category and makes sentence sense, you can allow some room for disagreement as to what's appropriate for each slot.

4 After they finish "Toon Time," students can check their answers and simultaneously reinforce their learning by completing "Toon Time": Additional Practice, pages 76–78. In this exercise, which is both an answer key for the Mad Libs activity and a practice sheet, students use a word bank to label sentence parts for the Mad Libs story.

5 You can check students' work on the Additional Practice exercise to gauge the extent to which they understand the uses of the parts of the sentence. As with other grammar practice activities, we encourage evaluating students' work but we discourage grading the product. (See Part V for a more complete discussion of assessment.)

6 Once you are satisfied that students understand the uses of the sentence parts, you can extend this lesson by challenging them to create their own stories, incorporating the parts of the sentence deliberately and appropriately. To get them going, give them a story starter and then have them work alone, in pairs, or in groups of three, to develop the story. (See page 79 for a model story starter.) Allow plenty of time for drafting, revising, and editing. The completed stories should be evaluated; Rubric Three on page 108 works well for this task.

Grammar Lessons You'll Love to Teach   Scholastic Teaching Resources

Toon Time

Section One

SENTENCE PARTS

of the soccer team   *the laughingstock of the school*   *despite his low grades*
the big joke of the whole school   *the king of the hill*

It was just too much for him. He, Roc Hansom, was _____ (*subject complement*). How had this happened to him? Wasn't he the most popular guy in school, the tall, dark, handsome captain _____ (*prepositional phrase*)? He was sure the guys admired him and the girls adored him, in part, he reasoned, because he was careful never to have a steady girlfriend. Play the field, spread the wealth, he thought. Even the teachers liked him, _____ (*prepositional phrase*), but hey, who had time for A's? Besides, with his movie-star looks and athletic talent, he figured he didn't need grades to be a success. He was _____ (*subject complement*). So what happened? How could he be _____ (*subject complement*)? Was someone trying to tell him something? These questions brought into focus the painful events of the past week.

Section Two

SENTENCE PARTS

Georgia Peach, the most gorgeous girl in school
to show off his orthodontically perfect white teeth   *hoping to find Rosetta Stone*
to follow her to a corner of the library

It all began last Monday in the library, a part of the school Roc rarely visited. He looked around the reading area, _____ (*participial phrase*), the big brain in Mrs. Clearwater's Earth Science class. He was sure Rosetta would help with his research project, probably even give him some of her work. Just then, _____ (*subject*), walked up to him.

"Hey, Roc," she cooed. "I've been looking for you. Wanna know a secret?"

"Uhhh, sure." He wanted to say something cool, but she had caught him off guard, so he just smiled _____ (*infinitive phrase*).

Georgia motioned for Roc _____ (*infinitive phrase*). "This is strictly top secret, so you've got to promise me you won't tell a living soul."

"No, no—not a soul. So what's the big secret?"

Section Three

SENTENCE PARTS

didn't wait for him to answer
smiled sweetly, glanced around the room, then leaned even closer to Roc
all of us on the committee   *this year's theme*   *you*

Georgia suppressed a little giggle as she moved closer to Roc. "Well, the winter dance

committee has decided that _____ *(subject)* will be cartoon characters.

How sweet is that?"

"Uhh, I guess, yeah, sweet."

Georgia _____ *(predicate)*. "We are all going to the dance as

cartoon characters. This formal dress stuff is sooooo yesterday. Don't you agree?" She

_____ *(predicate)*. _____ *(subject)* are really

psyched about this idea. We think it's awesome! And we're asking special people like you,

who have a lot of influence, to play along with us. It's gonna' be wicked fun! What do

_____ *(subject)* say?"

Section Four

SENTENCE PARTS

who will be who   *him*   *no to Georgia*   *his costume*
about Rosetta Stone and the research project   *exactly the right costume*

"Okay." How could he say _____ *(direct object)*? "So what

character should I be? Spiderman?" He was thinking how terrific he'd look in Spiderman's

muscle-revealing costume.

"We already have the costumes, but we haven't decided _____

(direct object). Don't worry, I'll make sure you have _____ *(direct*

object). And remember: not a word of this to anybody." She smiled reassuringly and hurried

out of the library.

By now Roc had forgotten _____ *(direct object)*. He was imagining

himself as Spiderman at the Snow Ball. Awesome!

By the day of the dance, Georgia had still not given _____ *(indirect object)*

_____ *(direct object)*. But when he asked her about it in homeroom,

she promised to deliver the costume to him at his house that evening. In fact, she said, she

would even pick him up.

Section Five

SENTENCE PARTS

what she was talking about   *let me see who you are*
what she described as a costume perfect for him   *who I thought I'd be*   *trust me*

She was as good as her word. She arrived carrying a large box containing

_____ (*dependent clause*). She urged him to hurry and change

into it.

He took the box, then noticed she was wearing a big cape over her costume. "Hey,

take off your cape and _____ (*independent clause*)."

She pulled the cape close around her, smiled, and said, "You'll see later. Just hurry

upstairs and change. We don't want to be late for the big surprise."

A few minutes later Roc came down dressed in his costume. "Georgia, are you sure

this is what I'm supposed to wear? It's not _____ (*dependent

clause*)."

"It's perfect for you, Roc." She flashed her drop-dead gorgeous smile.

_____ (*independent clause*); you'll be a sensation."

He figured she obviously knew _____ (*dependent clause*).

Roc pulled on his parka, and off they went to the Snow Ball.

Section Six

SENTENCE PARTS

everyone turned to stare at Georgia   *in a big, baggy Bugs Bunny costume*
felt frozen in place   *turned to laughter that reverberated off the polished walls*
his big bunny feet   *the dancing*

When they got to the school gym, decorated with large silver snowflakes suspended

from the ceiling, the DJ had already revved up the group and _____

(*subject*) had begun. But when Georgia and Roc walked in, the music stopped, the

dancing stopped, and _____ (*independent clause*), her cape

removed, in a party dress, and Roc, _____ (*prepositional phrase*),

complete with platter-big feet, tall, floppy ears, and black bunny nose. Nobody,

absolutely nobody else, was in a cartoon costume. The girls were in fancy dresses and

the guys in jackets and ties. For a moment the gym was silent, then the giggles

_____ (*predicate*). Everyone was laughing, even Georgia, all

laughing at him, the king of the hill, in this stupid bunny costume!

For several moments Roc _____ (*predicate*), like some stuffed

cartoon character, which he was. Finally, after the initial blow, he lifted _____

(*direct object*), ran out of the gym, and out of the school, all the way home.

Toon Time: Additional Practice

DIRECTIONS: Below is the Mad Libs story, "Toon Time," with the answers filled in. For additional practice, use the word banks to label the underlined answers with their correct sentence parts. Check the original story to see if your labels are correct. (The first underlined sentence part is done for you as a sample.)

Section One

SENTENCE PART LABELS

subject complement   subject complement   prepositional phrase
prepositional phrase   subject complement

subject complement
It was just too much for him. He, Roc Hansom, was <u>the laughingstock of the school</u>.

How had this happened to him? Wasn't he the most popular guy in school, the tall, dark, handsome captain <u>of the soccer team</u>? He was sure the guys admired him and the girls adored him, in part, he reasoned, because he was careful never to have a steady girlfriend. Play the field, spread the wealth, he thought. Even the teachers liked him, <u>despite his low grades</u>, but hey, who had time for A's? Besides, with his movie-star looks and athletic talent, he figured he didn't need grades to be a success. He was <u>the king of the hill</u>. So what happened? How could he be <u>the big joke of the whole school</u>? Was someone trying to tell him something? These questions brought into focus the painful events of the past week.

Section Two

SENTENCE PART LABELS

infinitive phrase   infinitive phrase   subject   participial phrase

It all began last Monday in the library, a part of the school Roc rarely visited. He looked around the reading area, <u>hoping to find Rosetta Stone</u>, the big brain in Mrs. Clearwater's Earth Science class. He was sure Rosetta would help with his research project, probably even give him some of her work. Just then, <u>Georgia Peach, the most gorgeous girl in school</u>, walked up to him

"Hey, Roc," she cooed. "I've been looking for you. Wanna know a secret?"

"Uhhh, sure." He wanted to say something cool, but she had caught him off guard, so he just smiled <u>to show off his orthodontically perfect while teeth</u>.

Georgia motioned for Roc <u>to follow her to a corner of the library</u>. "This is strictly top secret, so you've got to promise me you won't tell a living soul."

"No, no—not a soul. So what's the big secret?"

Section Three

SENTENCE PART LABELS

subject   *subject*   *predicate*   *predicate*   *subject*

Georgia suppressed a little giggle as she moved closer to Roc. "Well, the winter dance committee has decided that <u>this year's theme</u> will be cartoon characters. How sweet is that? "

"Uhh, I guess, yeah, sweet."

Georgia <u>smiled sweetly, glanced around the room, then learned even closer to Roc.</u>

"We are all going to the Snow Ball, the name we've given the dance, as cartoon characters. This formal dress stuff is sooooo yesterday. Don't you agree?" She <u>didn't wait for him to answer.</u> "<u>All of us on the committee</u> are really psyched about this idea. We think it's awesome. And we're asking special people, like you who have a lot of influence, to play along with us. It's gonna' be wicked fun! What do <u>you</u> say?"

Section Four

SENTENCE PART LABELS

direct object   *direct object*   *direct object*   *direct object*
indirect object   *direct object*

"Okay." How could he say <u>no to Georgia</u>? "So what character should I be? Spiderman?" He was thinking how great he'd look in Spiderman's muscle revealing costume.

"We already have the costumes, but we haven't decided <u>who will be who</u>. Don't worry, I'll make sure you have <u>exactly the right costume</u>. And remember: not a word of this to anybody." She smiled reassuringly and hurried out of the library.

By now Roc had forgotten <u>about Rosetta Stone and the research project</u>. He was imagining himself as Spiderman at the Snow Ball. Awesome!

By the day of the dance, Georgia had still not given <u>him</u> <u>his costume</u>. But when he asked her about it in homeroom, she promised to deliver the costume to him at his house that evening. In fact, she said, she would even pick him up.

Section Five

She was as good as her word. She arrived carrying a large box containing <u>what she described as a costume perfect for him</u>. She urged him to hurry and change into it. He took the box, then noticed she was wearing a big cape over her costume. "Hey, take off your cape and <u>let me see who you are</u>."

She pulled the cape close around her, smiled and said, "You'll see later. Just hurry upstairs and change. We don't want to be late for the big surprise."

A few minutes later Roc came down dressed in his costume. "Georgia, are you sure this is what I'm supposed to wear? It's not <u>who I thought I'd be</u>."

"It's perfect for you, Roc." She flashed her drop-dead gorgeous smile. "<u>Trust me</u>; you'll be a sensation."

He figured she obviously knew <u>what she was talking about</u>. Roc pulled on his parka, and off they went to the Snow Ball.

Section Six

When they got to the school gym, decorated with large silver snowflakes suspended from the ceiling, the DJ had already revved up the group and the dancing had begun. But when Georgia and Roc walked in, the music stopped, <u>the dancing</u> stopped, and <u>everyone turned to stare at Georgia</u>, her cape removed, in a party dress and Roc <u>in a big, baggy Bugs Bunny costume</u>, complete with platter-big feet, tall floppy ears, and black bunny nose. Nobody, absolutely nobody else was in a cartoon costume. The girls were in fancy dresses and the guys in jackets and ties. For a moment the gym was silent, then the giggles <u>turned to laughter that reverberated off the polished walls</u>. Everyone was laughing, even Georgia, all laughing at him, the king of the hill, in this stupid bunny costume!

For several moments Roc <u>felt frozen in place</u> like some stuffed cartoon character, which he was. Finally, after the initial blow, he lifted <u>his big bunny feet</u>, ran out of the gym, and out of the school, all the way home.

Grammar Lessons You'll Love to Teach Scholastic Teaching Resources

Use Your Imagination and Your Sentence Parts*

DIRECTIONS: Starting with the two paragraphs below, use your imagination to create a story. These two opening paragraphs provide you with a setting, some characters, and an inciting incident. Now you develop the plot, incorporate dialogue to give the characters some flesh and blood, build to a turning point, and conclude logically, perhaps with a surprise ending. In your story, try to use each of the sentence parts that you've learned. You may want to use the Mad Lib Grammatizator story, "Toon Time," as a model for the structure of your story.

It was a dark and stormy night when Oscar deSeuss, world- famous detective, found himself driving through dense fog on a remote peninsula of coastal Maine. His day had started far away in Ithaca, New York. Now he was exhausted from the long drive that had taken him through pouring rain to this dismal location. He wanted nothing more than a hot drink and a warm bed. What, he asked himself, had brought him to this miserable place, and especially on this particular day.

It had begun earlier in the week with a phone call from his old friend Estella von Moosehead. She was frantic, she said, and desperate for his help. Her darling Citronella had left the house as usual for her early morning walk through a forest of Maine pines to the rocky coast. She loved to climb among the giant boulders and savor the crashing waves' cold spray against her face. She had always returned from her solitary journeys in time for breakfast, but not on Wednesday. Of course Estella had searched for her and found not a trace. When she was still missing on Thursday, Estella called deSeuss begging for his help. He could not refuse the pleas of his old friend.

(Now you continue the story.)

*Note to teacher: This story starter can be used as an extended activity for Lesson III-7 or it can be used on its own as a writing and grammar practice activity.

PART IV

Growing Grammar Goodness: Lessons for Extending Learning

God is a verb.

—Buckminster Fuller

Have your students ever suffered from Grammar Aphasia? That's right, Grammar Aphasia—the all too common ailment characterized by students forgetting everything you ever taught them—from prepositions to predicates. Some students even suffer a total mind block at the mere mention of grammar. No recounting on your part of past teaching seems to jog their memories. So what to do?

We have to remember that grammar knowledge, like any other kind of knowledge, is retained only when it is interesting and relevant to the learner. So let's face it: We have to present the tools of grammar (parts of speech, sentence structure, usage, and punctuation) in contexts appealing to our students if we want that learning saved in the hard drives of their brains. That requires us to engage them in language activities that stimulate their imagination, have some relevance to their life, and provide an opportunity for positive feedback.

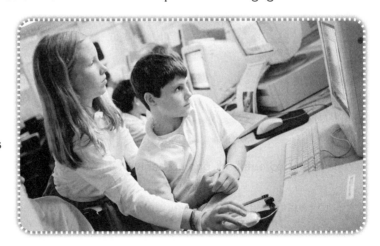

That's a tall order, but here we offer you four lessons that have captured the interest of a good many students, so we invite you to try them with yours.

Pondering Parts (of Speech) and Parts (of the Sentence) Painlessly: Diamonds, Triolets, and Cinquains

INTRODUCTION

Short, structured poems such as the *diamond*, *triolet*, and *cinquain* (pronounced *sing kane*) are popular poetic forms with which most students have had some experience. That familiarity helps get their attention. You can design the creation of any or all of these forms to focus on a topic that is simple enough for a child or sophisticated enough for an adult. You can also require that students incorporate specific grammatical elements in the construction of the poems.

PURPOSE

What students need to know and be able to do:

⊚ Understand the function of specific parts of speech and of the sentence

⊚ Know how to create structured poetic forms

⊚ Recognize poetry makes a statement about some aspect of the human condition

MATERIALS

⊚ Transparencies of model poems and of the poetry writing steps enumerated in Instructional Suggestions

Instructional Suggestions

Note: For this lesson, we walk you through an in-depth procedure for helping students create their own diamond poems. At the conclusion of this procedure, we describe characteristics of the other two poems, the triolet and the cinquain, and we provide models of those poems. You can modify the procedure for teaching diamonds and apply it to each of these other poetry forms.

1 Depending upon your students' background knowledge, either review or introduce the structured, seven-line poem known as the *diamond* (also called the *diamanté*). Explain that the name derives from the shape of the poem, which is a diamond. Draw a large diamond-shaped template on the board, or display a transparency of a diamond shape; see right.

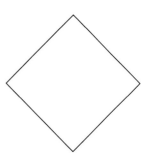

2 Tell students that in this lesson they will be writing their own diamond poems, according to specified criteria. But first you will show them a few model poems and you will ask them to help you analyze the elements of the poems so that by the time they are asked to write their own, they will be very familiar with the poem's characteristics and requirements. Using a transparency or the board, write out a model diamond poem. A sample is below:

Friend
Close, Dependable
Caring, Trusting, Loving
Someone, I thought, to be there for me
Lying, Betraying, Hurting
Resentful, Hateful
Enemy

3 Read the poem aloud, or call on a volunteer to read it aloud. Have students focus initially on the first and the last words of the poem. They will certainly recognize the opposites, *Friend* and *Enemy*. After students have identified these words as opposites, write on the board or a transparency:

Step 1: Choose two opposing nouns.

4 Next, have students focus on the second and sixth lines. They should realize that *Close* and *Dependable* describe *Friend* and that *Resentful* and *Hateful* describe *Enemy*. Now list the second step:

Step 2: Choose two adjectives that describe *Friend*.

5 Your next question should draw students' attention to the third and fifth lines. Students should note that these words each end in *–ing* and describe *Friend* and *Enemy* respectively. At this point you'll probably need to remind students that these *–ing* words are participles, specifically present participles. List the third step:

Step 3: Choose three present participles that describe *Friend*.

6 The fourth line presents more of a challenge. The writer can use this line to target different grammatical structures, typically a phrase or a clause. Invite students to explain what kind of structure they think *this* poem targets and what it tells readers. With a little help, they should see it is a clause (a dependent one) that says something about the friend. You might add, if they

don't, that it prepares readers for the change from *Friend* to *Enemy*. They will also need to note that it is the longest line in the poem and therefore creates two of the "points" of the diamond shape. Now list the fourth step:

Step 4: Create a phrase or a clause (independent or dependent) that says something about *Friend*.

7 Have students look again at the fifth line to deduce the next step. List this fifth step:

Step 5: Choose three present participles that describe *Enemy*.

8 Finally, direct students to look at the sixth line for the next step:

Step 6: Choose two adjectives that describe *Enemy*.

9 To reinforce students' knowledge about diamond poems, use the same procedure to walk them through a second model that incorporates a different grammatical element in line four—this time it's a phrase. A sample follows:

Dawn
Gold, Orange
Shining, Gleaming, Glowing
The transient source of energy and inspiration
Fading, Shrinking, Abandoning
Empty, Still
Dusk

10 Now students are ready to get going on their own poems. First, they'll need to brainstorm pairs of opposing nouns. You can do this as a whole class or by organizing students into partners. Consider using some of the vocabulary words from the books they are reading. For example, if a character is described as an *optimist*, ask students to identify his/her opposite—*a pessimist*. (Here's a way to incorporate word study and character study in your grammar activity.) Other opposing word combinations that can lead to interesting diamonds are *romantic and realist*; *slavery and freedom*; *cooperation and opposition*; *war and peace*; *truth and lies*; and *youth and age*.

Incidentally, if students offer pairs of adjectives—e.g., *kind and cruel*, help them convert the words into nouns: *kindness and cruelty*. If they come up with a pair like *good and bad*, allow that *good* and *bad* are generally used as adjectives, but they can be nouns in some contexts. Ask them to be more specific as to what they mean by "good" and "bad." At the same time, point out that vague designations like these can be very difficult to work with.

11 Once all students have decided on a pair of opposing nouns, invite them to create their own diamond poems. If the class needs more help, you might walk them through the steps together to create the poem. Whether they are generating their own poems or contributing to a teacher-guided class effort, encourage them along the way to experiment with words and to play with sounds and alliteration. Urge them to visualize a scene or a situation or a character and to try to put that image/idea into words so their readers can also envision it.

12 Ultimately the goal is to have students create several diamond poems, each using a different grammatical element in the fourth line, and to share the poems with classmates and friends. Once the poems are ready, you can use a computer to type them, print them out in color, and display them. Publishing in this way encourages attention to writing and adds relevance to the study of grammar.

Per Note on page 81, modify the procedure for diamonds for teaching students about triolets:

☉ The *triolet* is a French form of light verse that lends itself very easily to the creation of a poem requiring prepositional phrases and clauses, both independent and dependent. As with the diamond form, the triolet encourages experimentation—playing with words. The poem consists of eight lines, with lines one and two repeated as lines seven and eight. Line four is also line one repeated. Lines three and five rhyme with one, and line six rhymes with line two. Sounds a bit complicated, but it isn't really, as you can see from the enumerated steps and the model poem below:

> Line 1: Create a prepositional phrase(s).
> Line 2: Create a dependent clause.
> Line 3: Create an independent clause. (rhymes with line 1)
> Line 4: Repeat line 1.
> Line 5: Create a dependent clause. (rhymes with line 1)
> Line 6: Create an independent clause. (rhymes with line 2)
> Line 7: Repeat line 1.
> Line 8: Repeat line 2.

> On the day before vacation
> When students sit and stare
> There is no education
> On the day before vacation
> When teachers have no inspiration
> Their assignment books are bare
> On the day before vacation
> When students sit and stare

☉ The *cinquain* is a five-line poetic form in which each line has a prescribed number of syllables (not words). Line one has two syllables, line two has four, line three has six, line four has eight, and line five has two. You can use the form to encourage students to experiment with creating one simple sentence (an independent clause) that relies on modifying forms (adjective, participial phrases, and prepositional phrases) to convey the key image. The enumerated steps and two model poems follow:

Line 1: Create a two-syllable subject.
Line 2: Create a line of four syllables.
Line 3: Create a line of six syllables.
Line 4: Create a line of eight syllables.
Line 5: Create a line of two syllables.

The world
Is but a cup
Whose contents overflow
When people's greed like rushing rain
Is poured.

A plate
Of spaghetti
Piled in a great big mound
Inviting me to slurrrrp it down
Divine

Note that for all three forms of poetry, you can change the grammatical or syntactical requirement to suit your students' needs. Eventually, though, delete the syntactical requirements and set your students free to play with all three forms.

Participles for Lively Writing

INTRODUCTION

The reason Buckminster Fuller declared that "God is a verb" (page 77) is that verbs can do anything: They can even change form and act as a noun or an adjective or an adverb. When that happens, they become *verbals*. Verbals are words made from verbs—specifically *infinitives*, *gerunds*, and *participles*. Gerunds and infinitives act as nouns; participles act as adjectives and adverbs.

We especially like participles because they can infuse writing with drama and movement; they can make our imaginations dance. Not only that, but learning and understanding how to use participial phrases, as students do in this lesson, helps writers avoid misplacing modifiers that can result in confusing, awkward, even embarrassing sentences.

PURPOSE

What students need to know and be able to do:

- ⑥ Recognize present and past participles in their reading
- ⑥ Understand the function of participles
- ⑥ Incorporate participles and participial phrases in their writing

MATERIALS

- ⑥ Transparencies of model poems and of the poetry writing steps
- ⑥ Sports articles, collected from newspapers and sports magazines

Instructional Suggestions

1 Tell students that the focus of this lesson is the oft-misused but otherwise helpful and enlivening verb form called the *participle*. To help them understand the participle you will first explain it and provide examples of both its use and its abuse; then you will demonstrate how it can be used to liven up a special, formatted poem; and finally, you will give them a chance to write such poems themselves.

2 Explain to students that a participle looks like a verb, but it's only half a verb because by itself a participle cannot take a subject; it has to be partnered with a helping verb (e.g., *are, was, has been*) in order to function as a predicate in a sentence. It is thus a special verb form, considered part of a category called *verbals*. Participles are either in present or past form. On the board or a transparency, provide students with examples. Here is one sampling:

Verb	Present participle	Past participle
are cheering	cheering	cheered
had broken	breaking	broken
was eating	eating	eaten
is speaking	speaking	spoken

3 Explain further that being a "half-verb" does not limit the power of a participle. In fact, when used correctly in a sentence, this part of speech can be a dynamic adjective or an adverb. Sports writers and others who write about action use lots of participles and participial phrases. Read aloud or write the following example sentences for students:

> **Example sentence:** The *coaching* genius knows how quickly his reputation can be *tarnished*.

> **Explanation:** The present participle *coaching* describes the genius, and the past participle *tarnished* describes his reputation.

Frequently, participles are used most effectively as part of phrases—called, logically enough, *participial phrases*.

> **Example sentence:** *Screaming with frustration*, the angry fans rushed onto the soccer field.
> **Explanation:** The participial phrase *Screaming with frustration* adds to the description of the fans.

> **Example sentence:** Antoine Winfield's *crunching* tackle sent the ball *flying end-over-end toward the end zone*.
> **Explanation:** The present participle *crunching* describes Winfield's tackle, and *flying end-over-end toward the end zone* is a participial phrase that describes the motion of the ball.

4 Next illustrate for students how participles are often misused and abused in writing. Many students have probably already met up with this dreaded grammar error—the misplaced participial modifier. On the board or a transparency, present the following samples of misplaced participial modifiers (shown in italics in the example sentences) and have some fun in the process as students recognize how silly the sentences sound.

> **Example sentence:** *Hissing and yowling in the tree*, the fireman tried to rescue the cat.
> **Comments:** This sounds like the fireman was hissing and yowling in the tree.

> **Example sentence:** The baby was delivered and handed to the pediatrician, *breathing and crying immediately*.

Comments: Was the pediatrician breathing and crying immediately? That's odd.

Example sentence: The neighbor's lawnmower was reported *stolen by the police*.
Comments: Oh, my gosh, the police stole the lawnmower! Could that be right?

Example sentence: *Lying on the beach all day,* her mother was afraid Ursaline would get sunburned.
Comments: If her mother were really the one lying on the beach all day, why would Ursaline be at risk of a sunburn?

Example sentence: *Flying over New York City at night,* the Empire State Building looked like a welcoming beacon of light.
Comments: Could the Empire State Building be flying over the city?

The problem with all but the last sentence is that the writers have failed to put the participial phrases close to the nouns they are modifying, so the intended meaning gets garbled. In the last sentence, the writer failed to provide a noun or pronoun for the participial phrase to modify, so the phrase is dangling, unattached to anything—unless, of course, the writer really meant that the Empire State Building was flying over the city at night! Once you have discussed the sentences (and we hope had a few chuckles in the process), explore with students ways to rewrite the sentences to get the participles where they belong.

5. Make available to students copies of newspapers and sports magazines. Invite them, either with partners or in small groups, to browse through sports articles to find examples of participles in action. Have partners or groups share their examples with the whole class.

6. Now share with students examples of *shaped* (sometimes called "concrete") poems. Typically these poems capture and graphically reflect a pattern of motion or activity. Thus, many sports lend themselves to shaped poetry. In shaped poems the poet relies on both the shape that the poem forms and specifically on participles, which describe action, to help him or her convey the drama and movement of the sport.

7. To help students prepare for writing their own shaped poems, present one or more model poems for them to read and analyze. A sample shaped poem, inspired by the poet's watching an Olympic skier attack moguls, is shown at the end of this lesson, page 89.

8. Ask students to comment on the shape of the poem. What does the zigzag pattern illustrate? Make sure that they are able to see how the action described in the poem is mirrored by the poem's shape. Ask them to identify the participles and participial phrases: *packed* powder, *competing against himself, sure of success, sliding, slipping, succumbing.* Call their attention to the alliteration in the poem (the repeated *s* sound). How does this repetition of sound add to the poem's effect? Note: If you would like to provide further examples of shaped poems, we recommend the following: "The Sidewalk

Grammar Lessons You'll Love to Teach Scholastic Teaching Resources

Racer" by Lillian Morrison (skateboarding); "Alone in the Nets" by Arnold Adoff (soccer); and "Constantly Risking Absurdity" by Lawrence Ferlinghetti (aerial acrobatics).

9   Finally, give students the opportunity to experiment with creating their own shaped poems. Begin by having them brainstorm a list of sports they enjoy playing or watching. Here are some sports that students might not include but that work well for this type of poetry: hiking, ice skating, dancing (a very athletic activity), and surfing. As students draft their poems, remind them to use participles and participial phrases and encourage them to select alliterative words, if appropriate.

10   Follow up the first round of writing by having students write shaped poems about topics other than sports. Here are some possibilities: the movements of a particular animal, a child at play, a house painter at work, a pizza maker, or a grocery clerk. Actually, any animal or person whose activity catches a student's attention and is characterized by a certain pattern of motion could make an excellent topic. In the process of creating these poems, students are playing with language, creating images, and discovering the expressive power of participles in their writing.

Downhill Racer
A swish
        breaks
                the silence
                        of the frozen slope,
                                the skier skims
                        the surface
                of the packed powder,
                        strong sinews overreach themselves.
He strives
        for speed,
                competing
                        against
                                himself,
                                strong,
                                sure of
                        success,
                                he swoops
                                        down
                                        the slope,
                                        sliding,
                                slipping,
                        succumbing,
        to the tyranny of silent snow.

Appositives for Sentence Applause

INTRODUCTION

Imagine the paragraph below as something dashed off by one of your students in response to an assignment "to describe an amusing incident with your best friend."

George

My best friend is a dog. He is a black hound dog. He has big feet and big floppy ears. My dad says he has a talent for trouble. His name is George. I don't think he knows his name is George. The reason is because my mom doesn't like George to chew the furniture. She yells at him all day no, no, bad dog. I think maybe he thinks that's his name.

Does this piece give you *agita* because of its redundancies but at the same time give you a chuckle? There's something about this anecdote that makes a teacher just want to reach out to help the writer clean up the syntax and focus on the humor. There's no point in telling the student to combine some of the sentences; a writer at this developmental stage in the composing process would probably string some of the clauses together in a run-on and connect the rest with *and*. Our approach is to introduce writers to the *appositive* as a way to make their writing more fluent, more focused, and more readable.

Perhaps your heart hasn't beat joyfully at the sight of an appositive in quite a while. Well, following this lesson, you just might have a classroom of students eager to convert simple, perhaps simplistic, redundant sentences to modifying noun phrases or clauses, deliberately placed "in apposition to" a noun. So, be still your beating heart, take a deep breath, and get ready for some joyful appositive moments.

PURPOSE

What students need to know and be able to do:

- Recognize the difference between main ideas in sentences and descriptive details that make the main idea more interesting or vivid

- Use appositives in sentences

- Combine simple, repetitive sentences to avoid unnecessary redundancies, be more specific, and create more fluent writing

- Learn how to punctuate appositives

⊚ Transparencies of modeled material

⊚ Practice activity, pages 93–94

Instructional Suggestions

1 Tell students that this lesson is all about *appositives*. Assure them that this grammatical element is not as mysterious as it might sound. In fact, soon they'll feel as comfortable with the word *appositive* as they are with the word *preposition*. And in order to help start them off, you'll teach them the lyrics to "The Apposition Song" (see below). Have them add this to their growing repertoire of Grammar and Snacks Club songs and cheers. Students may not know what all the words mean yet, but they will soon, and for now they can just have fun with the song, complete with head movement for emphasis.

> **The Apposition Song**
> (sung to the tune of the 1944 Bing Crosby hit, "Accentuate the Positive")
>
> You got ta ac cen tuate appositives
> *(You gotta accentuate the positive)*
>
> E lim minate redundancies
> *(Eliminate the negative)*
>
> Latch on to specificity
> *(Latch on to the affirmative)*
>
> and don't mess with commas in between.
> *(And don't mess with Mister In-Between)*

2 Write the paragraph "George" (see Introduction to this lesson) on a transparency or the board. Read it aloud with the class. Ask students what information is stated in the first sentence and what role this sentence plays. (It's the main idea: "My best friend is a dog.") Now have students identify what kind of information is provided by the next three sentences (descriptions of the writer's best friend). Model how you experiment revising this paragraph by connecting the main idea to the descriptive information. The new sentence could look like this:

> My best friend is a dog, a black hound with big feet, floppy ears, and a talent for trouble.

3 Now ask students to compare the new sentence with the original story. Guide students to understand the advantages of combining these four sentences. Help them see that you got rid of wordy redundancies and a string of short, choppy, sentences by linking up interesting information about the dog in one sentence. Explain that because the descriptive information provides details

but is not absolutely essential to the main idea, it is set off from what it describes by commas. Call attention to "a black hound with big feet, floppy ears, and a talent for trouble" and label it as an appositive—that is, a word or phrase that modifies a noun.

4   Now have students identify what we learn in the next four sentences—that George doesn't know his name and why. Following the procedure described in steps 2 and 3, modeling for students how you combine sentences—in this case, five sentences into two. Here's what the two new sentences might look like:

> I named him George, but I don't think he knows that because my mom, who doesn't like George to chew on the furniture, yells at him all day, "No, no, bad dog." I bet he thinks NoNoBadDog is his name.

5   In addition to focusing on the new appositive and on making the same points about eliminating choppiness and redundancies, you can use this revision to highlight a few additional angles about the decision making involved in writing. Point out, for instance, that in the last sentence you changed *I think maybe* to *I bet* to avoid a repetition of the word think. And if no one brings it up, ask students if they can figure out why you repeated the words *NoNoBadDog*. Explain that you did so because you wanted to distinguish between the mom's invective and what the dog understands his name to be. Also, *NoNoBadDog* is the punch line, so you decided to "punch it up." You made a stylistic decision. All writers do that; it's their prerogative.

6   Now that students have gotten their feet wet, or at least damp, with appositives, it's a good idea to offer them a reinforcement exercise. A sample assignment is provided on pages 93–94. Note: In addition to this exercise, which targets appositives, you might want to offer your students further practice in streamlining their writing. Two such practice activities are provided in the Appendices, pages 124 and 125.

7   By now your students should be aware how much more fluent their writing will sound when they streamline it by using appositives, so you can encourage them to use these modifiers when they are drafting and/or revising their compositions. For a while, you may still have to point out the information that could be effectively restructured as a noun phrase or clause, but more than half the battle has been won: Students now have models of appositives they can emulate. So be prepared for a positive joy in the classroom!

Grammar Lessons You'll Love to Teach   Scholastic Teaching Resources

Choosing Appositives

DIRECTIONS: Revise the following material by combining each group of sentences into one sentence. Use appositives wherever it's appropriate. You may add connecting words (such as conjunctions or prepositions) if necessary. Note that you may need or wish to change the order of the listed details as well as the forms of some of the verbs. Remember to eliminate redundancies.

a. Fleetwood raced up to the classroom door.

b. He was sweating.

c. He was out of breath.

First new sentence: _____

_____.

a. He was late to class.

b. This was not the first time.

c. He was sure Mrs. Pumpkin would give him detention for life.

Second new sentence: _____

_____.

a. He stood at the door.

b. He was very still.

c. He put his hand on the doorknob.

d. He peered through the window.

Third new sentence: _____

_____.

a. He saw Miss Peach.

b. He was ecstatic.

c. Miss Peach was the substitute teacher for the school.

Fourth new sentence: _____

_____.

a. Fleetwood heaved a sigh of relief.

b. He loved Miss Peach.

c. Everyone loved Miss Peach.

Fifth new sentence: _____

_____.

   a. He turned the doorknob.

   b. He smiled his broadest smile.

   c. He entered the classroom.

   Sixth new sentence: _____

_____.

Now write your complete paragraph on the lines below.

_____

_____

_____

_____

_____

_____

_____

_____

ANSWERS

Fold under on the dotted line. Do NOT peek until you have completed the practice page!

(Remember, these answers are only suggestions. There may be more than one way to combine these sentence groups and still incorporate appositives.)

1. Sweating and out of breath, Fleetwood raced up to the classroom door.

2. Because he was late to class, not for the first time, he was sure Mrs. Pumpkin would give him detention for life.

    or

    He was sure Mrs. Pumpkin would give him detention for life because he was late for class, not for the first time.

    [Note: Either of the above ways is correct as long as the dependent clause, *because he was late to class, not for the first time*, is connected to the independent clause, *he was sure Mrs. Pumpkin would give him detention*.]

3. Standing very still at the door, he put his hand on the doorknob and peered through the window.

4. When he saw Miss Peach, the substitute teacher for the school, he was ecstatic.

5. Fleetwood heaved a sigh of relief because, like everyone, he loved Miss Peach.

6. Turning the doorknob and smiling his broadest smile, he entered the classroom.

Grammar Lessons You'll Love to Teach Scholastic Teaching Resources

Cultivating Clause Control

INTRODUCTION

Have you ever been so frustrated with students writing in fragments that you've decided it's time to launch, again, into a lesson on clauses? Once and for all, you reason, your students will understand the difference between a dependent and an independent clause. So be it!

You begin by trying to determine what they may already know about clauses, perhaps asking directly, "What do you know about clauses?" A likely student answer will be: "There are two of 'em, Santa Claus and his missus." Not exactly the answer you hoped for, but you did get a response you can work with, once you stop giggling.

"Okay," you reason, kind of. "Let's say one Claus, maybe Santa, is the *dependent* Claus. He can't function by himself; he needs help from the elves, the reindeer, and the missus. That means Mrs. Claus is the *independent* one who functions by herself. After all, Santa's often away and she's the one who keeps the North Pole stable, the home fires burning, and the elves working."

You could continue with the metaphor, but your point is made: The independent clause stands alone as a complete sentence. The dependent clause is just that, dependent on the independent clause.

Once you have clause definition under control, albeit abstractly, students need to use clauses themselves consciously in their writing. Here you'll find some structured-writing clause-control activities you can use for instruction and as models for additional lessons and activities. The goal, as ever, is to put students in control of their writing, which also strengthens their reading skills.

PURPOSE

What students need to know and be able to do:

- ⑨ Understand the structure and function of independent and dependent clauses

- ⑨ Know when to use each kind of clause appropriately

- ⑨ Learn to write "found poems"

- ⑨ Recognize that many forms of poetry make a statement about some aspect of the human condition

☺ Transparencies of model poems and selected instructional material

☺ A variety of materials to use in brainstorming for found poems (see step 4)

Instructional Suggestions

1   Tell students that this lesson focuses on clauses—both independent and
    dependent. After learning more about clauses, they will have an opportunity
    to create a special kind of poetry, called "found poems," that is based on
    other written material. In their found poems they will make use of their new, or
    renewed, knowledge about clauses.

2   Review with students that an independent clause is simply a complete
    sentence; it has a subject and a predicate and can stand alone. A dependent
    clause also has a subject and a predicate but cannot stand alone.

    Example sentence: Pandora opened the box that she had found in the
    cupboard.

    Explanation: The first clause, *Pandora opened the box*, is an independent
    clause because it can stand alone as a complete sentence. The second
    clause, *that she had found in the cupboard*, can't stand alone; it has to be
    attached to the independent clause. Thus, it is a dependent clause.

    Present this second example on a transparency or the board so that students
    can analyze it:

    The space explorers returned to Earth with living creatures that they had
    found on the planet Krypton.

    Ask students to tell you which clause is independent and which is dependent. If
    they need help, review with them that the signal for the dependent clause is the
    relative pronoun *that*. In fact, help students realize that they can recognize
    dependent clauses because they usually begin with a relative pronoun, such *as
    that*, *which*, *who*, *what*, etc., or with a linking conjunction, such as *when*, *after*,
    as if, *until*, *because*, etc. To review the various subordinators and functions of
    dependent clauses further, send your students to their grammar handbooks.

3   The next step is to help students use dependent clauses as adjectives and
    adverbs appropriately. Explain that with these modifiers there's a kind of
    hierarchy of use. Sometimes, putting a modifying idea in a clause makes it
    especially important to the sentence, maybe more so than it should be. The
    result can be a wordy sentence. On a transparency or the board write the
    following example:

    When Cleo's kayak capsized into waters that were icy cold, she lost her
    paddle, which left her stranded in lonely Crick Cove, which was off the coast
    of Maine, until a young fisherman, who was handsome, rescued her.

Use this sentence to demonstrate the process a writer can use to tighten and focus her or his writing. Explain that what the writer needs here is to decide which ideas are most important. In this case, it is Cleo's being stranded in lonely Crick Cove without her paddle. So that idea needs to go into an independent clause. Then the writer decides what the next most important ideas are—probably Cleo's boat capsizing and her rescue by a fisherman. Those ideas can go into dependent clauses. The idea that the waters are off the coast of Maine is next in order of importance and can be expressed in a prepositional phrase. The icy condition of the water doesn't need a clause or a phrase, only the adjective *icy*. Neither does the demeanor of the fisherman need a clause or a phrase, only the adjective *handsome*. The revised sentence could read like this:

dependent clause with three prepositional phrases
When Cleo's kayak capsized in the icy waters off the coast of Maine,

independent clause with a compound predicate
she lost her paddle and was left stranded in Crick Cove

dependent clause
until a handsome young fisherman rescued her.

Help students to realize that the independent clause, which is the heart of this sentence, does not come first in the sequence of clauses. In interesting writing, the order of independent and dependent clauses varies greatly within and among sentences.

Enough talking *about* clauses. As we consistently advocate, it's critical to get your students involved in writing activities that give them the opportunity to make deliberate use of grammar, as in the next steps.

4 Tell students that before you ask them to create their own "found poems," you'll provide them with a model, which you'll examine together. But first of all, you need to define this genre for them. Explain that found poetry allows a poet to write about almost anything and to use other writers' words and phrases—legally! It's a lot like playing with "Magnetic Poetry" kits, except that instead of magnetic bits, writers use paper and scissors or the cut-and-paste option on the computer. Here are additional characteristics:

ⓖ Most basically, it is the reshaping of other writers' language into original poems.

ⓖ Sources can be found just about anywhere—in newspaper articles, appliance or sports equipment instructions, game directions, even textbooks.

ⓖ It can rhyme and have a specific rhythm, but it does not have to.

5 Using a transparency, present the sample found poem on page 98. Tell the class that the student who wrote this poem created it using words found in the preface of a first-year Latin textbook.

Learning a Language

The future of Latin in the United States
Relies on this book

Enlightened upper grades in our elementary school have
All rights reserved
@1969 Longman

Even those who recognize the wisdom
Of justification

Our own experience in school
Was bad

So we want to make it
As bad for you

Here in the most difficult
To understand Latin Book
Ever written

Have FUN
And remember

Modern Languages
don't mean anything.
LATIN IS LIFE.

by Sam Sack, age 13

Words taken from the preface to *Preparatory Latin Book 1: 2nd Edition* by William Buehner and John Ambrose. New York, NY: Longman, 1977.

6 After reading the sample poem aloud with the class and discussing further what makes it a found poem, help students to identify the independent and dependent clauses in the poem. Point out that because this is a free-verse poem, the writer chose not to punctuate the clauses as he would if he had been writing prose. Ask students where they would have placed periods and commas to make the dependent and independent clauses easier to recognize. (The stanza composed of lines 6 and 7 is a dependent clause. Each of the other stanzas is an independent clause.)

7 Now it's time for students to try writing their own found poems. Before they begin creating their original poems, brainstorm with them possible sources. It will help the brainstorming process if you make available ahead of time a variety of materials—for example, directions for playing a computer game or Pictionary, Scattagories, or Scrabble; instructions for the care and feeding of a gerbil, kitten, or puppy; preparations for a camping expedition; or magazine and newspaper articles (especially from science sections and special interest magazines) about personal experiences and special events. We've found the *Defenders of Wildlife* magazine to be a particularly rich source; we include an excerpt from this magazine on page 100.

Grammar Lessons You'll Love to Teach Scholastic Teaching Resources

8   Once all students have chosen a piece of writing to work from, follow these simple rules:

   ⊚ Have them copy, by hand or on the computer, several words, phrases, and clauses that seem most important to the subject of the piece or that express a particularly interesting concept.

   ⊚ Next, have students begin to arrange these selected words, phrases, and clauses into new forms, including independent and dependent clauses, labeling each as to its type.

   ⊚ Encourage students to alter verb tenses, switch singular and plural endings, and change pronouns to resolve gender reference and other problems. Tell students they can repeat lines, words, or phrases as they see fit, and insert or change punctuation to help the reader understand the meaning.

   ⊚ Remind students to include the source of the words for their found poem by citing the information in a reference note. (See the example on page 98 for a model.)

9   Allow students sufficient time to play with the words, phrases, and clauses they select to create their found poems. Encourage revision by modeling the process as you create your own found poem(s) along with the class.

10   Because both the study of clauses and the creative products students generate in this lesson are time-intensive and challenging, you might choose to evaluate the poems. Rubric Two (page 107), which you can adapt to assess students' understanding and control of clauses, will work well for evaluating the found poems.

11   As students complete their found poems, encourage them to enhance their work with original illustrations. Celebrate their success by displaying the poems in your classroom and/or creating a bound collection of the pieces to be placed in the school library. You might even hold a reading and advertise it in the school newspaper.

Learning How to Follow a Tuna*

Built for speed, the bluefin tuna is the sports car of the sea, from its sleek, two-toned metallic blue and silvery white body to the hefty price it commands—$50,000 or more for a prime specimen. Not surprisingly, this delicacy is relentlessly pursued by fishing fleets worldwide and is becoming increasingly scarce. A new study suggests that the way bluefin stocks are managed is contributing to their decline.

Researchers from Stanford University and the Monterey Bay Aquarium captured hundreds of bluefin tuna along the Atlantic Coast, tagged them with electronic tracking devices and mapped their movements. They confirmed that the North Atlantic has two populations of bluefin, an eastern stock that breeds in the Mediterranean Sea and a more seriously depleted western stock that spawns in the Gulf of Mexico. But they also discovered that these two groups, currently managed separately, regularly intermingle as they zip back and forth across the Atlantic to feed.

"Electronic tagging provides the best scientific information we've ever had to properly manage these tuna," says Barbara Block, the marine biologist who headed the tagging study. "We must, as an international community, start to act responsibly to ensure the future of this species."

Excerpted from *Defenders of Wildlife* magazine, Summer 2005.

*Note to teacher: This passage is suitable for use as source material for students' creation of found poems as described in Lesson IV-4.

PART V

(Grammar Goodness) Guide to Assessment and Evaluation

Only in grammar can you be more than perfect.

—William Safire

You know the scenario. You assign a reading or writing task, a research or grammar practice activity and the inevitable question follows: "Does this count? Are you gonna grade this?" You wince, not so much because you intend to dodge the question, but because so many students consider every "school" task as something to be done only for a grade, never to simply learn important information or valuable skills.

The answer to the question "Does this count?" is "No" when it is asked about grammar practice work. Grades aren't even considered for learning the

Decoder List skills and maintaining the Personal Skills Record, or for guided practice on language tasks that reinforce those skills. On the other hand, the answer to the question is "Yes" when it's asked about the products (both written and spoken) that students compose and create. Here we discuss both kinds of situations and distinguish them for you, as well as offer several rubrics you can use for work that does "count."

Assessment and Evaluation Are Two Related but Distinct Processes

FIRST OFF, WE SHOULD ACKNOWLEDGE THAT—LIKE MANY TERMS IN education—different people use the related terms *assessment* and *evaluation* in somewhat different ways. We'll lay out what we mean by the terms and go from there.

What Assessment Is All About

We define assessment as a formative, ongoing process that teachers use to inform instructional decisions, reflect specific outcomes, and provide feedback to students. The goal is to help both teachers and students appreciate students' growth as language users and to determine what students still need to learn. Effective assessment is at its core a matter of day-to-day informal information gathering and keen observation of regular learning situations, such as practice activities and classroom participation.

Grades are no more appropriate for these kinds of learning activities than for basketball clinic practice, warm-up exercises, or drop-shot tryouts. These routines are necessary pre-game practices so that when the real game begins, the athletes can play well and have a good chance of winning. During all the practice work, the coach is, in fact, engaged in assessment—observing the players' strengths, their skills development, and their readiness for the game.

You, the English language arts teacher, are the grammar coach, constantly assessing your students' skills development and language strengths to determine the extent of their growth as competent readers, writers, and speakers. Assessment for all coaches, whether of grammar or sports, is the process of determining the extent to which your students have mastered the concepts and competencies of the game. For the English teacher/grammar coach that means the extent to which students can:

- Understand the vocabulary of grammar.

- Correctly use the parts of speech and parts of the sentence to speak and write clearly, coherently, and purposefully.

- Apply their understanding of English language structure to read mature, grade-appropriate texts for meaning and even insight.

Just to underscore these points, let's say you have a student who doesn't grasp the difference in use between subjective and objective pronouns. The effective response is to provide more direct teaching and guided practice to help him learn what he needs to know to be a competent language user. The same goes for the girl in the next row who is having trouble with dependent and independent clauses. And so on. What these students don't need is a grade for their learning efforts. But there is a right time for grading, and we discuss that next.

What Evaluation Is All About

We define *evaluation* as a summative process aimed at assigning a value to what students have learned. What they have learned is demonstrated by a particular product that reflects their application of understandings and skills. Another way of stating this is that the product reflects the extent to which students have mastered what they have practiced. This product is given a grade—a grade determined by criteria for mastery that have been clear to students from the beginning of the learning process and all during the weeks and months of practice.

The products take many formats, both written and spoken. These demonstrations can be poems, stories, essays, mini-plays, reviews, analyses, news stories, speeches, interviews, media presentations, and so on. These authentic compositions are the real thing, just as basketball games and other sports events are the real thing for athletes. Unlike practice sessions, games are played for scores; the same is true for students' language products.

The Role of Rubrics

CREATING RUBRICS MAY SEEM DIFFICULT INITIALLY, BUT TEACHERS WHO use them regularly (and this includes both of us) recognize that the very process of creating them helps us as teachers to focus on what our students need to know and be able to do. The rubrics also help students understand what they need to learn and be able to do. We believe in involving students themselves in the evaluation process of their mastery products. Thus, for each of the steps below we include students as much as possible in the creation of the rubrics.

In this section, we walk you through the process of creating a particular rubric, Rubric One, and then provide an example of this rubric (page 106). Following that example, you'll find two alternative formats for rubrics, with brief commentary.

Determining the Task to Be Evaluated

We find task-specific rubrics to be useful for the very reason that they are so focused on a particular, identified product. Once you determine that your students are far enough along in their learning about a particular language or grammar subject to be evaluated, you can come up with a task for this evaluation. Involve students in the choice of the specific task. For example, if they have completed a good deal of work on prepositional poems, you and they together might come up with a task that requires them to create a themed collection (five or six, perhaps) of prepositional poems. From the moment the task is assigned, students are aware that their product will ultimately be evaluated via a task-specific rubric. In fact, the next step is to determine with them the nature of that rubric.

Determining and Defining the Qualities to Be Evaluated

Based on what students have learned from their practice work on, for example, creating prepositional poems, we now need to decide, with them, what *qualities* are important enough to be included in the rubric. Considering the context, they are likely to volunteer "form" and "language use" and "grammar." You can nudge students along, if necessary, and suggest these additional categories: "content" (sometimes called "meaning"), "development," and "organization." Help them streamline ahead of time and suggest that, for the purposes of the rubric, "form" can be folded within "content." (It's worth noting that there are no hard and fast rules. You'll need to adapt each rubric somewhat to address the specific task and situation. For example, we've found that it's sometimes appropriate to include "development" and "organization" within the "content" category as well, but for this example, we have retained it as a separate quality.)

The next step is to help students define what each of these qualities really means and how the meaning can be stated clearly enough to lend itself to evaluation. Allow sufficient time for you and your students to create definitions that are appropriate for the task and understood by everyone. Don't be afraid to use the vocabulary of evaluation; give your students the opportunity to become familiar with the language teachers use to evaluate students' work.

A sample set of definitions for these qualities follows:

> **Content:** The extent to which the response is appropriate to the task
>
> **Development:** The extent to which ideas and images are specific and relevant to the subject of the task
>
> **Organization:** The extent to which the response exhibits direction, shape, and coherence
>
> **Language Use:** The extent to which the response reveals an awareness of purpose and effective use of words (if you decide to highlight spelling as an instructional goal that will be graded, this would be the place to do so)
>
> **Grammar:** The extent to which the response is grammatically correct

Note that if you decide to include punctuation, spelling, and usage with grammar as one quality, you can rename the quality "conventions." However, because the focus of attention here is on grammar in a literary context, it often works best to identify grammar as a separate quality to be evaluated.

Determining and Defining the Levels of Response

Once you have decided on the qualities appropriate for the task assigned, you need to decide on the levels of response for your rubric. We often use a four-level rubric, with 3 (A or Excellent) representing a high score; 2 (B or Good) a middle score; 1 (C or Adequate) a low score; and 0 indicating the meaning is not clear or the response is not relevant to the assignment. We generally don't give a letter grade below C on these grammar-based activities; rather, we give the student some teaching support and another opportunity to complete the assignment. Some teachers prefer a five-level rubric, which breaks down as follows: 4 (A or Excellent) is the highest grade; followed by 3 (B or Good) and 2 (C or Adequate). A grade of 1 acknowledges the student's effort to fulfill the assignment. A 0 still indicates that a response is not clear or relevant to the assignment.

After determining the levels of response, you and your students need to define those levels in clear, descriptive language. Avoid evaluative terms—e.g., "good," "excellent," or "poor"—in your descriptions. Instead, describe the student's performance for each category.

Rubric One

You can use this kind of rubric to grade your students' pieces holistically, that is, to give an overall grade for the product. You can also circle those level-of-response descriptions on each rubric that reflect a student's work. That way the student can see what he or she has done well and where he or she needs to improve. In other words, the holistic grade is explained.

A few more words of explanation. It's important to realize that your holistic score is not necessarily determined by adding the number of 3's, 2's, and 1's and then dividing them by five (or however many qualities you identify for evaluation). That procedure can result in a skewed grade, one not reflective of the extent to which the student has demonstrated her or his understanding of the task and the skills being measured. In fact, you may weight some qualities more than others. For example, with a story response *content* and *development* might be given more weight than *grammar*. With a poem, *language use* and *organization* might be more heavily weighted. Or, if correct use of pronouns has been a major focus of an assignment, *grammar* might be more weighted. Then again, you may decide to give equal weight to all qualities.

It all depends on what you have emphasized in your teaching and in the assignment. So here's where your good teacher judgment comes into play. By circling the most accurate descriptions of responses to the evaluation qualities, you indicate to students their strengths and weaknesses, but then you make an overall, i.e., holistic, judgment of their performance.

A sample of this rubric is shown on page 106.

Name of student _____			Overall grade _____	
Qualities to be evaluated	**3** Responses at this level	**2** Responses at this level	**1** Responses at this level	**0** Responses at this level
Content: The extent to which the response is appropriate to the task	Fulfills all the requirement of the task Reflects clear, thematic idea	Fulfills most of the requirement of the task Thematic idea not always clear	Fulfills few of the requirements of the task	The response is not relevant to the assignment
Development: The extent to which ideas and images are specific and relevant to the subject of the task	The images are relevant, clear and appropriate to the thematic idea	Most of the images are clear and appropriate to the topic Some relevance to the thematic idea	Few images with little relevance to the thematic idea	The response is not relevant to the assignment or it is unclear
Organization: The extent to which the response exhibits direction, shape, and coherence	Establishes and maintains a clear focus Follows a logical sequence of ideas	Is generally focused, but some irrelevant details Shows a clear attempt at organization	Does not establish and maintain a focus Shows little or no organization	No evidence of focus or organization
Language use: The extent to which the response reveals an awareness of purpose and effective use of words	Is fluent and easy to read Uses vivid and appropriate language	Is easy to read Uses appropriate language	Is readable Uses some appropriate language	Meaning is not clear
Grammar: The extent to which the response is grammatically correct	The piece is grammatically correct for the task	The piece is generally correct for the task	The piece is minimally correct for the task There are errors in parts of speech and/or parts of the sentence	The piece demonstrates a lack of understanding of the parts of speech and the parts of the sentence

Rubric Two

An example of another rubric format you may prefer is given on page 107. Rubric Two works well particularly for the recipe poem and the shaped poem, or for any other less structured/more expressive work. This kind of more loosely structured rubric eliminates numbers (unless you choose to incorporate them) and encourages holistic evaluation in broad strokes—e.g., Excellent, Good, and Adequate. The students whose work isn't "adequate" should be encouraged to try again with help, of course, to achieve at least an "adequate" overall grade.

If you wish, you can assign a percentage to each quality on this rubric, weighting certain

Grammar Lessons You'll Love to Teach Scholastic Teaching Resources

qualities as appropriate for the assignment, and determine the final grade arithmetically. However, we encourage the holistic approach.

A few words about the final two items on this rubric. The *Commendations* block is the place to include your positive comments about the student's work—what you especially liked in the piece, what the student is doing well, or how he or she is showing improvement. The *Recommendations* block is a dedicated space for you to offer suggestions about how the student can improve his or her response. Of course, the understanding is that revisions are encouraged! The commendations and recommendations you offer should help all students build on their achievements and be guided toward success in their revisions.

Name of student _____ Overall grade _____

Qualities to be evaluated	Excellent	Good	Adequate
Content:			
Focus of the language topic			
Clarity (and appropriateness) of the images			
Knowledge of the subject			
Development:			
Fully developed idea			
Specific, relevant details			
Organization:			
Logical flow, from beginning to end			
Engaging			
Language use:			
Appropriate and effective use of targeted language elements			
Commendations:			
Recommendations:			

Rubric Three

Here we present another rubric model. This one works well for products focusing on sentence building—e.g., activities that provide practice on parts of the sentence, because it specifically targets the task at-hand, selection of details, and language use. Like Rubric Two, this rubric also works well for holistic scoring. Note that the descriptions we provide in this model are general; you will probably want to make them more task-specific. Just be sure to describe performance levels objectively. The numbers listed in the left-hand column are the evaluative levels, which you can circle and also label with evaluative language if you wish—Excellent, Good, Adequate, or Incomplete.

Name of student _____ Overall grade _____

		Comments
4	**Complete fulfillment of the task** Consistently correct and varied sentence structures Relevant and engaging details Logical development Sophisticated use of language Consistently correct language mechanics	
3	**Fulfillment of the task** Generally correct sentence structures Relevant details Correct use of language A few errors in mechanics, but none that interfere with meaning	
2	**Some effort to fulfill the task** Some correct sentence structures, but inconsistent Few details, and some that are irrelevant Generally correct use of language Some errors in mechanics that may interfere with meaning	
1	**Failure to complete the task** Few correct sentence structures Few details Inaccurate use of language Errors in language mechanics that interfere with meaning	

Regardless of the products you choose for your evaluations or the rubrics you create to measure your students' learning, make sure you have given them plenty of guided practice and that they understand the criteria by which their mastery work will be graded. In this way, grading becomes part of the learning process and an effective way for you to communicate to your students and their parents the extent of each student's learning.

CLOSING THOUGHT

We sincerely hope this book has helped you in your efforts to promote grammar goodness in your students' lives. May you continue to nurture young readers, writers, and thinkers by empowering them with knowledge and skills in the tools and techniques of our dynamic language. We salute the bold, brave, and committed teachers who convey the power of language to their students by teaching them grammar with humor as well as academic rigor. As a result, many young speakers and writers will communicate, enlighten, and inspire their audiences with elegance and eloquence—and they will be able to do so for life.

APPENDICES

Grammar Lessons You'll Love to Teach   Scholastic Teaching Resources

Practice for Pronoun Power!

DIRECTIONS: Remember that the object of a preposition always takes objective case (*him, her, us, them, whom*), while the verb *to be* and other linking verbs take subjective case (*I, she, he, who, we, they*). Underline the correct pronoun in each sentence. On the line below the sentence, write an explanation for your choice. (Hints: For all the asterisked items, add a verb to finish the sentence in your head. For all the items that are questions, first turn the question into a statement.) The first one is done as an example.

1. In the story of Demeter, it is (<u>she</u>/her) who is upset that her daughter has been abducted.

    she = subjective case; subject complement of linking verb *is*

2. Hercules performed the Twelve Labors, and it was (he/him) who slew the Hydra.

    _____

3. On the playing field, Ophelia is as skilled as (he/him).*

    _____

4. The coach gave my friend more advice on training than (I/me).

    _____

5. Because we stopped at the burger place, we were less hungry than (they/them).*

    _____

6. The coaches were as happy about the win as (us/we).*

    _____

7. Mrs. Crahbahpple offered Ophelia as well as (he/him) extra help on pronouns.

    _____

8. Is Ivan as smart as (her/she)?*

    _____

9. Ivan was more excited about the game than (them/they).*

    _____

10. To (who/whom) did he turn for help when he could not do the homework?

    _____

11. (Who/Whom) did you meet at Ophelia's party?

    _____

12. (Who/Whom) was it that spilled all that soda?

_____

13. (Who/Whom) got first prize?

_____

14. With (who/whom) did Hercules fall in love?

_____

15. (Whom/Who) did Zeus kill for flying the sun chariot too close to Earth?

_____

16. The young man (who/whom) you met at my party was my brother.

_____

17. Lois Lowry is an author (who/whom) has received much acclaim.

_____

18. She is an author (who/whom) I would love to meet.

_____

19. She is the one (who/whom) wrote _The Giver_.

_____

20. Was it Lois Lowry (who/whom) also wrote _Gathering Blue_?

_____

21. The speaker informed the group and (I/me) about rockets.

_____

22. Call Susie and (he/him) when you decide on the movie.

_____

23. In the story of Snow White, it is (she/her) who is treated cruelly by her stepmother.

_____

24. This is between you and (I/me), but I really did not study for this test!

_____

25. It was a scary day for Ophelia and (she/her).

Grammar Lessons You'll Love to Teach   Scholastic Teaching Resources

ANSWERS to Practice for Pronoun Power!

Do NOT peek until you have completed the practice page!

1. she = subjective case; subject complement of linking verb *is*

2. he = subjective case; subject complement of linking verb *was*

3. he = subjective case; subject of the sentence you must complete in your head: ". . . as he *is skilled.*"

4. me = objective case; indirect object of the sentence you must complete in your head: ". . . than *he gave* me."

5. they = subjective case; subject of the sentence you must complete in your head: ". . . than they *were hungry.*"

6. we = subjective case; subject of the sentence you must complete in your head: ". . . as we *were happy.*"

7. him = objective case; compound indirect object

8. she = subjective case; subject of the sentence you must complete in your head: ". . . as she *is smart.*"

9. they = subjective case; subject of the sentence you must complete in your head: ". . . as they *were excited.*"

10. whom = objective case; object of the preposition *to*

11. whom = objective case; direct object. Turn the question into a statement: *You did meet whom at Ophelia's party.*

12. who = subjective case; subject complement of linking verb *was*

13. who = subjective case; subject of the sentence

14. whom = objective case; object of the preposition *with*

15. whom = objective case; direct object

16. whom = objective case; direct object of the dependent clause

17. who = subjective case; subject of dependent clause *who has received*

18. whom = objective case; direct object of infinitive phrase *to meet*

19. who = subjective case; subject of the dependent clause *who wrote* <u>The Giver</u>

20. who = subjective case; subject of the dependent clause *who also wrote* <u>Gathering Blue</u>

21. me = objective case; compound direct object

22. him = objective case; compound direct object

23. she = subjective case; subject complement of the linking verb *is*

24. me = objective case; compound object of the preposition *between*

25. her = objective case; compound object of the preposition *for*

Label Parts of the Sentence

INITIAL DIRECTIONS: Before completing the six sentences for this practice sheet, which are all based on the Harry Potter books, study the sample sentence and follow the directions just below it.

Sample: Wood threw Angelina the Quaffle.

Label the sentence by using your Definitions: Parts of the Sentence handout (pages 54–55) and recite out loud:

a. *Threw* is the predicate of the sentence because it shows action.

b. *Wood* is the subject because it is a noun or a pronoun and the predicate *threw* is telling what the subject does.

c. *Quaffle* is the direct object because it completes the predicate. Wood threw what? Wood threw the Quaffle.

d. *Angelina* is an indirect object because it tells to whom the predicate *threw* was done. Wood threw to whom? Wood threw to Angelina.

Here is how the sentence looks when it has been labeled:

subject	predicate	indirect object	direct object
Wood	threw	Angelina	the Quaffle.

DIRECTIONS: Label the following sentences. Remember that a sentence is only required to have a subject and a predicate. Whether or not other parts of a sentence are included depends on the intention/meaning of the sentence. When a sentence has more than one of the same part, add the word *compound*. For example, sentence 4 has two predicates, so *cheered* and *shouted* should be labeled *compound predicate*.

WORD BANK FOR PARTS OF THE SENTENCE:

predicate   compound predicate   subject   compound subject
direct object   compound direct object   indirect object

1. Angelina missed it.

2. Hermione screamed.

3. Harry caught the Snitch.

4. Hermione cheered and shouted.

5. Harry and Ron smiled.

6. Harry laughed and tossed Hermione his broom.

- -

ANSWERS

Fold under on the dotted line. Do NOT peek until you have completed the practice page!

    subject predicate direct object
1. Angelina   missed   it.

    subject   predicate
2. Hermione screamed.

    subject predicate direct object
3. Harry   caught   the Snitch.

    subject   compound predicate
4. Hermione   cheered and shouted.

    compound subject predicate
5. Harry and Ron   smiled.

    subject compound predicate   indirect object   direct object
6. Harry   laughed and tossed   Hermione   his broom.

Label Parts of the Sentence

INITIAL DIRECTIONS: Before completing the six sentences for this practice sheet, which are all based on the Harry Potter books, study the sample sentence and follow the directions just below it.

Sample: Wood threw Angelina the Quaffle across the field.

Label the sentence by using your Definitions: Parts of the Sentence handout (pages 54–55) and recite out loud:

a. *Threw* is the predicate of the sentence because it shows action.

b. *Wood* is the subject because it is a noun or a pronoun and the predicate *threw* is telling what the subject does.

c. *Quaffle* is the direct object because it completes the predicate. Wood threw what? Wood threw the Quaffle.

d. *Angelina* is an indirect object because it tells to whom the predicate *threw* was done. Wood threw to whom? Wood threw to Angelina.

e. *Across the field* is a prepositional phrase formed by the preposition *across* and the noun *field*, which is the object of the preposition.

Here is how the sentence looks when it has been labeled:

subject	predicate	indirect object	direct object	prepositional phrase
Wood	threw	Angelina	the Quaffle	across the field.

DIRECTIONS: Label the following sentences. Remember that a sentence is only required to have a subject and a predicate. Whether or not other parts of a sentence are included depends on the intention/meaning of the sentence. When a sentence has more than one of the same part, add the word *compound*. For example, sentence 4 has two predicates, so *cheered* and *shouted* should be labeled *compound predicate*.

WORD BANK FOR PARTS OF THE SENTENCE:

predicate	compound predicate	subject	compound subject
direct object	compound direct object	indirect object	prepositional phrase

1. It sailed past Angelina's hand.

2. Hermione screamed during the match.

3. Harry caught the Snitch in his left hand.

4. Under her umbrella, Hermione cheered and shouted.

5. Harry and Ron smiled with their widest grins.

5. Harry laughed and tossed his broom into the stands, in Hermione's direction.

ANSWERS

Fold under on the dotted line. Do NOT peek until you have completed the practice page!

    subject *predicate*   *prepositional phrase*
1. It   sailed   past Angelina's hand.

    subject   *predicate*   *prepositional phrase*
2. Hermione   screamed   during the match.

    subject *predicate*   *direct object*   *prepositional phrase*
3. Harry   caught   the Snitch   in his left hand.

    prepositional phrase   *subject*   *compound predicate*
4. Under her umbrella, Hermione cheered and shouted.

    compound subject *predicate*   *prepositional phrase*
5. Harry and Ron   smiled   with their widest grins.

    subject   *compound predicate*   *direct object*   *prepositional phrase*   *prepositional phrase*
6. Harry   laughed and tossed   his broom   into the stands,   in Hermione's direction.

Label Parts of the Sentence and Parts of Speech

INITIAL DIRECTIONS: Before completing the six sentences for this practice sheet, which are all based on the Harry Potter books, study the sample sentence and follow the directions just below it.

>**Sample:** Wood threw Angelina the Quaffle across the field.

Label the sentence by using your Definitions: Parts of the Sentence handout (pages 54–55). Using the Definitions: Parts of Speech handout (pages 47–49), do the same for parts of speech, writing the parts of speech labels below the sentence. Recite aloud the following statements:

>a. *Threw* is the predicate of the sentence because it shows action.
>
>b. *Wood* is the subject because it is a noun or a pronoun and the predicate *threw* is telling what the subject does.
>
>c. *Quaffle* is the direct object because it completes the predicate. Wood threw what? Wood threw the Quaffle.
>
>d. *Angelina* is an indirect object because it tells to whom the predicate *threw* was done. Wood threw to whom? Wood threw to Angelina.
>
>e. *Across the field* is a prepositional phrase formed by the preposition *across* and the noun *field*, which is the object of the preposition.

Here is how the sentence looks when it has been labeled:

subject	predicate	indirect object		direct object	prepositional phrase		
Wood	threw	Angelina	the	Quaffle	across	the	field.
noun	*verb*	*noun*	*article*	*noun*	*preposition*	*article*	*noun*

DIRECTIONS: First, label the parts of the sentence <u>above</u> the sentence. Remember that a sentence is only required to have a subject and a predicate. Whether or not other parts of a sentence are included depends on the intention/meaning of the sentence. When a sentence has more than one of the same part, add the word *compound*. For example, sentence 4 has two predicates, so *cheered* and *shouted* should be labeled *compound predicate*. Second, label the parts of speech <u>below</u> the sentence.

WORD BANK FOR PARTS OF THE SENTENCE:
(Remember: Write these above the sentence.)

>predicate   compound predicate   subject   compound subject
>subject complement   direct object   compound direct object   indirect object
>prepositional phrase   dependent clause

WORD BANK FOR PARTS OF SPEECH:
(Remember: Write these below the sentence.)

>noun   pronoun   adjective   article   verb
>adverb   preposition   conjunction

1. It sailed past Angelina's hand.

2. Hermione screamed during the match.

3. Harry's Nimbus Two Thousand spun in midair and screamed across the field.

4. He dodged the Bludger and grabbed the golden Snitch.

5. Harry's friends raced to the field and cheered for Harry.

6. They lifted Harry high on their shoulders and carried him in triumph.

ANSWERS

Fold under on the dotted line. Do NOT peek until you have completed the practice page!

```
        subject   predicate              prepositional phrase
 1. It            sailed       past    Angelina's    hand.
    noun          verb      preposition  poss. noun   noun

        subject       predicate        prepositional phrase
 2. Hermione      screamed      during    the    match.
     noun            verb       preposition article noun

        subject                    compound pred.  prep. phrase       compound pred.    prep. phrase
 3. Harry's   Nimbus Two Thousand     spun         in  midair     and screamed      across the  field.
    poss. noun      noun              verb         prep. noun      conj.  verb       prep. article noun

        subject   comp. pred.   dir. obj.       comp. pred.         dir. obj.
 4. He         dodged      the Bludger   and grabbed      the  golden Snitch.
    Pron.        verb       art. noun     conj.  verb       art.  adj.   noun

        subject          comp. pred.      prep. phrase       comp. pred.      prep. phrase
 5. Harry's  friends      raced         to  the  field   and  cheered      for Harry.
    Poss.noun noun         verb         prep. art. noun   conj.   verb       prep. noun

        subj.  comp. pred.  dir. obj.            prep. phrase          comp. pred dir. obj.  prep. phrase
 6. They    lifted      Harry       high    on    their    shoulders   and carried    him    in   triumph.
    pronoun  verb        noun       adverb  prep. poss. pron.  noun     conj.  verb    pron.  prep.  noun
```

Famous First Lines From Best-Sellers

DIRECTIONS: Each sentence below is the opening line of a famous novel. First, label the parts of the sentence above each sentence. Then label the parts of speech below each sentence. (Do not label the book titles and author names in parentheses; these are the sources for the quotations.) Use the word banks to help you remember the terms. The first item is completed for you to use as an example.

WORD BANK FOR PARTS OF THE SENTENCE:
(*Remember: Write these above the sentence.*)

predicate**   compound predicate**   subject**   compound subject**

direct object   compound direct object   indirect object

prepositional phrase   subject complement   object complement

(** **Note:** *For the purposes of this exercise, the terms* predicate, compound predicate, subject, *and* compound subject *should be written above only the simple subject (main noun or pronoun) and predicate (main verb and any helping verb.)*

WORD BANK FOR PARTS OF SPEECH:
(*Remember: Write these below the sentence.*)

noun   adjective   pronoun   possessive pronoun

article   verb   adverb   preposition   conjunction

subject	predicate				subj. complement	
1. "It	was	a	dark	and	stormy	night."
pronoun	*verb*	*article*	*adj.*	*conj.*	*adj.*	*noun*

(from *A Wrinkle in Time*, by Madeleine L'Engle)

2. "It was a bright, cold day in April, and the clocks were striking thirteen."

(from *1984*, by George Orwell)

3. "Call me Ishmael."

(from *Moby Dick*, by Herman Melville)

4. "It was seven minutes after midnight."

(from *The Curious Incident of the Dog in the Night-Time*, by Mark Haddon)

5. "The *Nellie*, a cruising yawl, swung to her anchor without a flutter of the sails, and was at rest."

(from *Heart of Darkness*, by Joseph Conrad)

6. "Kino awakened in the near dark."

(from *The Pearl*, by John Steinbeck)

7. "We didn't always live on Mango Street."

(from *The House on Mango Street*, by Sandra Cisneros)

8. "For the first fifteen years of our lives, Danny and I lived within five blocks of each other

and neither of us knew of the other's existence."

(from *The Chosen*, by Chaim Potok)

BONUS WRITING PROMPT: Use one of the sentences above to start a story or poem of your own. Be sure to give credit to the original author by placing the sentence in quotation marks and marking it with an asterisk (*). Cite the title and author of the original work (under your title or at the end of your piece).

ANSWERS

Fold under on the dotted line. Do NOT peek until you have completed the practice page!

subj.   pred.   subj. complement
1. "It   was   a   dark   and   stormy   night."
pronoun verb article adj. conj. adj.   noun

subj. pred.   subj. complement   prep. phrase   subject   pred.   dir. obj.
2. "It   a   bright, cold day   in   April,   and the   clocks   were striking   thirteen."*
pron. verb   article adj.   adj. noun prep. noun conj. art.   noun   verb   verb   noun

   *Note: *This is a compound sentence; it is two complete sentences joined by the conjunction and.*

   (the subject of this sentence, you, is implied)
   pred. dir. obj. obj. comp.
3. "Call   me   Ishmael."
   verb   pronoun   noun

subj. pred.   subj. comp.   prep. phrase
4. "It   was   seven minutes   after midnight."
pron. verb   adj. noun   prep. noun

   subject   appositive   compound pred.   prep. phrase   prep. phrase   prep. phrase
5. "The Nellie,   a cruising yawl,   swung   to   her   anchor   without a flutter   of   the   sails,
   art. noun   art. adj.   noun   verb   prep. poss. pron. noun   prep. art. noun   prep. art. noun

       comp. pred   subj. comp.
   and   was   at   rest."
   conj.   verb   prep. noun

   subj.   predicate   prep. phrase
6. "Kino   awakened   in   the   near   dark."
   noun   verb   prep. art. adj.   noun

   subj.   complete predicate   prep. phrase
7. "We   didn't   always live   on   Mango Street."
   pronoun verb ("did")+ adverb (" 'nt" = "not") adverb verb prep.   noun

   prep. phrase   prep. phrase   comp. subject   pred.   prep. phrase   prep. phrase
8. "For the first fifteen years   of   our   lives,   Danny and I   lived   within five blocks   of each other
   prep. art. adv. adj. noun prep. poss. prn. noun   noun conj. pron. verb   prep. adj. noun   prep. adj. noun

       subj. prep. phrase pred.   prep. phrase
   and neither of   us   knew   of   the   other's   existence."*
   conj. pronoun prep. pronoun verb   prep. art. poss. adj.   noun

   Note: This is a compound sentence; it is two complete sentences joined by the conjunction and. The first sentence contains compound subjects.

Phrase Craze

DIRECTIONS: Believe it or not, each of the sentences below has one ordinary subject, predicate, and sometimes a direct object, subject complement, or appositive; every other sentence part is a prepositional phrase. Your job is to label the underlined parts of each sentence. Use the word bank to choose terms. (Do not label the source information in parentheses.) You'll see that elegant—and even funny—writing is part of a phrase craze!

WORD BANK FOR PARTS OF THE SENTENCE:
(Remember: Write these above the sentence.)

subject   predicate   direct object   appositive
subject complement   prepositional phrase

1. I pledge allegiance to the flag

   of the United States of America, and to the republic

   for which it stands, one nation, under God, indivisible,

   with liberty and justice for all.
   (The Pledge of Allegiance to the American flag)

2. Over the river and through the woods to Grandmother's house we go.
   (from the 1884 poem, "Thanksgiving Day," by Lydia Marie Child))

3. Among twenty snowy mountains

   The only moving thing

   Was the eye of the blackbird.
   (From the poem, "Thirteen Ways of Looking at a Blackbird" by Wallace Stevens)

4. The loss of her husband had had a profound effect on Angeline Fowl.
   (from Chapter One of Artemis Fowl: The Arctic Incident, by Eoin Colfer)

5. I take a two-hour nap, from one o'clock to four.
   (Yogi Berra)

ANSWERS to Phrase Craze

Do NOT peek until you have completed the practice page!

   subject   *predicate*   *direct object*   *prep. phrase*   *prep. phrase*
1. I   pledge   allegiance   to the flag   of the United States

    prep. phrase   *prep. phrase*   *prep. phrase*   *appositive*
    of America   and   to the republic   for which it stands,   one nation,

    prep. phrase   *prep. phrase*   *prep. phrase*
    under God,   indivisible,   with liberty and justice   for all.

(Note: In case you are wondering about the two lonely words without labels: and *= conjunction;* indivisible *= adjective that modifies the appositive* nation.*)*

   prep. phrase   *prep. phrase*   *prep. phrase*   *subject* *predicate*
2. Over the river   and   through the woods   to Grandmother's house   we   go.

      prepositional phrase
3. Among twenty snowy mountains

       subject
  The only moving thing

predicate *subject complement* *prepositional phrase*
 Was   the eye   of the blackbird.

   subject   *prep. phrase*   *predicate*   *direct object*
4. The loss   of her husband   had had   a profound effect

   prepositional phrase
  on Angeline Fowl.

 subject *predicate*   *direct object*   *prep. phrase* *prep. phrase*
5. I   take   a two-hour nap,   from one o'clock   to four.

Revising *Wonderland*: Varying Sentence Patterns and Eliminating Redundancies

DIRECTIONS: Each group of numbered sentences below makes up one sentence in a paragraph in Lewis Carroll's *Alice in Wonderland*. We have taken Carroll's original sentences apart and separated them into the shorter sentences you see here. Your job is to try to put it all back together! Combine each group of sentences to form one sentence, using appositives, conjunctions, or punctuation to create compound sentences (two or more sentences connected by conjunctions or semicolons) or complex sentences (sentences with at least one independent clause and one dependent clause or phrase). Feel free to cut words and/or add connectives. After you have finished, see if your version is close to Lewis Carroll's (below).

1. Alice was beginning to get tired of sitting on the bank.
2. She was tired of having nothing to do.
3. Suddenly a white rabbit with pink eyes ran close by her.
4. There was nothing so remarkable about that.
5. Alice did not think it much out of the way to hear the rabbit say to itself, "Oh dear! Oh dear! I shall be late!"
6. But when the rabbit actually took a watch out of his waistcoat pocket, he looked at it.
7. Then he hurried on.
8. Alice started to her feet.

Write your revised version here:

_____

_____

_____

_____

_____

_____

_____

Original paragraph from *Alice in Wonderland*: *Alice was beginning to get tired of sitting on the bank and of having nothing to do . . . when suddenly a white rabbit with pink eyes ran close by her. There was nothing so very remarkable in that; nor did Alice think it so very much out of the way to hear the rabbit say to itself, "Oh dear! Oh dear! I shall be late!" But when the rabbit actually took a watch out of his waistcoat pocket, looked at it, and then hurried on, Alice started to her feet.*

Bonus Writing Prompt: Try replacing all of the nouns and verbs in Carroll's paragraph with words of your own choosing. (Example: "Ezekiel *was* starting *to get* fed up with standing *on the* sidewalk *and of* thinking random things . . . *when suddenly a* gray ferret *with* white ears scurried *close by him* . . .") You can learn a lot from modeling your sentence structure after a master craftsman, and you might even start a new story that you want to continue!

Grammar Lessons You'll Love to Teach Scholastic Teaching Resources

Revising *The Red Badge of Courage*: Varying Sentence Patterns and Eliminating Redundancies

DIRECTIONS: Each group of numbered sentences below makes up one sentence in a paragraph in Stephen Crane's *The Red Badge of Courage*. We have taken Crane's original sentences apart and separated them into the shorter sentences you see here. Your job is to try to put it all back together! Combine each group of sentences to form one sentence, using appositives, conjunctions, or punctuation to create compound sentences (two or more sentences connected by conjunctions or semicolons) or complex sentences (sentences with at least one independent clause and one dependent clause or phrase). Feel free to cut words and/or add connectives. After you have finished, see if your version is close to Stephen Crane's (below).

1. The cold passed reluctantly from the earth.
2. The retiring fogs revealed an army stretched out on the hills.
3. The army was resting.
4. The landscape changed from brown to green.
5. The army awakened.
6. It began to tremble with eagerness at the noise of rumors.
7. It cast its eyes upon the roads.
8. The roads were growing from long troughs of liquid mud to proper thoroughfares.
9. A river purled at the army's feet.
10. It was amber-tinted in the shadow of its banks.

Write your revised version here:

_____

_____

_____

_____

_____

_____

_____

Original paragraph from *The Red Badge of Courage*: *The cold passed reluctantly from the earth, and the retiring fogs revealed an army stretched out on the hills, resting. As the landscape changed from brown to green, the army awakened, and began to tremble with eagerness at the noise of rumors. It cast its eyes upon the roads, which were growing from long troughs of liquid mud to proper thoroughfares. A river, amber-tinted, in the shadow of its banks, purled at the army's feet.*"

Bonus Writing Prompt: Try replacing all of the nouns and verbs in Crane's paragraph with words of your own choosing. (Example: "*The* rain moved *reluctantly from the* yard, *and the* retiring moon highlighted *a* dark shape, *lurking...*") You can learn a lot from modeling your sentence structure after a master craftsman, and you might even start a new story that you want to continue!

BIBLIOGRAPHY

Resist the temptation to buy one of each! After all, you're on a teacher's salary.

Kid-Friendly Texts and Resources

Berbrich, Joan. *Laugh Your Way Through Grammar.* New York, NY: Amsco School Publications, Inc., 1990.

This book uses lots of humor as well as clear and thorough explanations. It is set up in an unusual way. In the first section of the book, students work through practice session pages, and each sentence is followed by a number code. The number code leads the student to the page in the grammar text in the second section containing the rule or lesson on the mistake in that sentence. The book is designed for traditional classroom use, as well as for independent study. (www.amscopub.com)

Christopher Lee Publications. *English Grammar Flipper Study Guide* and *Punctuation and Capitalization Flipper Study Guide.* South Bend, IN: Christopher Lee Publications, 2000.

These are cool-looking mini-reference guides that consist of laminated file cards mounted on a hard backing so that the flat page of the cards fits into a three-ring binder. Topics appear at the top of the cards for easy reference. (www.medinalogos.com/homeschooling)

Elliott, Rebecca. *Barron's Painless Grammar.* Hauppauge, NY: Barron's Educational Series, 1997.

The cover of this book reads: "If you think grammar is dull and boring, open this book—and think again! An enjoyable, completely painless examination of parts of speech, sentence construction, and punctuation. And you'll laugh at down-to-earth examples that show you the difference between good and bad grammar." The comical illustrations are irresistible, and chapters include "Brain-Ticklers" or mini-quizzes for review and practice (answer keys included in the book). (www.barronseduc.com)

Fine, Edith H., and Josephson, Judith P. *Nitty-Gritty Grammar: A Not-So-Serious Guide to Clear Communication* and *More Nitty-Gritty Grammar: Another Not-So-Serious Guide to Clear Communication.* Berkeley, CA: Ten Speed Press, 1998; 2001.

Students really like these books. The explanations are clear and concise, examples are funny (kids actually giggle when reading them), and there are plenty of grammar-related comic strips and cartoons. It does not include exercises, so you must supplement it with a workbook. Grammar for Life (see below) is a good choice for a workbook to pair with Nitty-Gritty Grammar. This way the students get humor in the text and grade-level content enrichment in the workbook practice pages. (www.tenspeed.com)

Holt, Rinehart and Winston. *Warriner's High School Handbook.* Chicago, IL: Holt, Rinehart and Winston, 1992.

An American classroom standard for more years than we can remember, Warriner's is thorough and clear in its explanations and extensive exercises. This book is used as a classroom text in the old tradition, with separate answer keys and more tests available for purchase. The downside is that it lacks any humor and the language style is very formal, so students are not eager to revisit this book. (www.hrw.com)

Loyola Press. *Exercises in English: Grammar for Life.* Chicago, IL: Loyola Press, 2003.

There are four levels in this workbook series, and they roughly correspond to grades 6, 7, 8, and 9. Each page contains a short summary of a rule, concept, or skill with examples, and plenty of practice exercises that are based on grade-appropriate literature, science, and social studies topics. The highest level is perfectly appropriate for use in grades 9 through 12. (www.loyolabooks.org; 1-800-621-1008)

Lubell, Marcia, and Townsend, Ruth. *Language Works.* Cincinnati, OH: South Western Educational Publishing, 1993.

Great for grades 9–12, this unique workbook engages students as proofreaders and editors throughout an imaginary author's journey to publication. E-mail ruthtstory@mindspring.com for purchasing information.

Grammar Lessons You'll Love to Teach   Scholastic Teaching Resources

Miller Thurston, Cheryl. *How to Avoid English Teachers' Pet Peeves: Improve Your Writing by Eliminating the Common Errors That English Teachers See Most Often.* Fort Collins, CO: Cottonwood Press, 2001.

> This is a very user-friendly book in shape and size (160 pages, 7 inches square), as well as approach. Each "English Teachers' Pet Peeve" is briefly described and explained in jargon-free language on one or two pages, with a few practice examples at the end of each chapter and overall reviews as well. (www.cottonwoodpress.com; 1-800-864-4297)

Princeton Review. *Grammar Smart*, 2nd edition. New York, NY: Random House, 2001.

> Incorporating The Princeton Review's irreverence and humor in its approach to learning, this book offers solid instruction and practice. High school students definitely enjoy the tone of this book. (www.review.com)

Risso, Mario. *Safari Grammar* and *Safari Punctuation.* Lincolnwood, IL: Passport Books; NTC/Contemporary Publishing, 1989.

> The humorous comic-strip adventures of Jungle Jack keep students in grades 6 through 9 laughing as they practice and learn grammar elements and skills.

Write Source Educational Publishing House. *Writers Inc.* Burlington, WI: Write Source Educational Publishing House, 2000.

> This is a very comprehensive handbook of grammar and usage, as well as writing conventions and practices. Sprinkled with fun and kid-friendly comics-style illustrations, this handbook is very thorough. (1-800-445-8613)

Teacher Resources

Atwell, Nancie. *In the Middle: Writing, Reading, and Learning with Adolescents.* Portsmouth, NH: Boynton/Cook, 1987.

> This book has become a classic for middle school teachers. Atwell's methods have been changing English/Language Arts teaching for the better for many years, and they continue to do so. Her workshop approach to reading and writing is built on a strong foundation of pedagogically sound, student-centered systems of process and principles.

Bell Kiester, Jane. *Caught'Ya!: Grammar With a Giggle.* Gainesville, FL: Maupin House Publishing, 1990.

> Kiester incorporates a classic error hunt with a sentence-a-day approach to teach basic grammar skills in context. This book includes stories for elementary, middle, and high school students and enough sentences for the entire school year. (www.maupinhouse.com ; 1-800-524-0634)

Gordon, Karen Elizabeth. *The Deluxe Transitive Vampire: A Grammar Handbook for the Innocent, the Eager, and the Doomed.* New York, NY: Pantheon Books, 1993.

> This book's cover correctly states that Gordon "spins a lively gothic narrative with such characters as the Debutante, famous courtesan, wolf, bat, vampire, pizza chef . . . with a uniquely wicked, witty, and playful style. Yet every rule is explained with clarity and precision." (www.randomhouse.com/pantheon)

Hacker, Diane. *A Writer's Reference*, 5th edition. New York, NY: Bedford/St. Martin's Press, 2003.

> Often used as a college text, this $50 comprehensive handbook includes cross-references referring readers to relevant sections on its companion Web site. It offers 1,000 electronic exercise items for grammar, research, and writing. (www.bedfordstmartins.com)

Halverson, Jim. *Grammar Works! Grades 4–8.* New York, NY: Scholastic Inc., 1996.

> A textbook for teachers with 15 reproducible skills lessons, Grammar Works! teaches essential grammar rules. Games and graphics will appeal to the younger middle-schooler. (www.scholastic.com; 1-800-SCHOLAStic)

Haussamen, Brock with Amy Benjamin, Martha Kolln, and Rebecca S. Wheeler. *Grammar Alive! A Guide for Teachers.* Urbana, IL: National Council of Teachers of English, 2003.

> This book is a collection of essays and chapters by different professionals and veterans in the business of teaching and writing. Approaches vary, and topics range from diagramming sentences to dealing with nonstandard English and "homespeak." There is also a grammar glossary and annotated list of sources. (www.ncte.org; 1-877-369-6283)

Noden, Henry R. *Image Grammar: Using Grammatical Structures to Teach Writing*. Portsmouth, NH: Heinemann, 1999.

> This book's cover says it all: "*Image Grammar is based on the premise that a writer is much like an artist who 'paints' images, using grammatical structures as tools.*" Includes CD with lessons and samples. (www.heinemann.com

O'Conner, Patricia T. *Woe Is I: The Grammarphobe's Guide to Better English in Plain English*, 2nd edition. New York, NY: Riverhead Books (Penguin Group), 2004.

> An enjoyable and accessible narrative, Woe Is I leads the reader through common errors, explains how they come about, and clarifies their corrections. (www.penguin.com)

Robb, Laura. *Grammar Lessons and Strategies That Strengthen Students' Writing, Grades 4-8*. New York, NY: Scholastic Inc., 2001.

> This is a text for the teacher filled with many excellent lesson plans and student-friendly reproducibles. (www.scholastic.com; 1-800-SCHOLAStic)

Sams, Lynn. "How To Teach Grammar, Analytical Thinking, and Writing: A Method That Works." Urbana, IL: NCTE: *English Journal* (Jan. 2003), p. 57.

Truss, Lynn. *Eats, Shoots & Leaves: The Zero Tolerance Approach to Punctuation*. New York, NY: Gotham Books (Penguin Group), 2004.

> As the book flap states, Lynn Truss tells the world in her "urbane, witty and very English way," where we have gone wrong in areas of punctuation and how we must fix things straightaway. This bestseller has its readers smiling, but it can sometimes seem confusing and inconsistent due to unstated differences in British and American pronunciation rules. (www.penguin.com)

Weaver, Constance. *Teaching Grammar in Context*. Portsmouth, NH: Heinemann, 1996.

> Weaver gives an overview of the history and theories of teaching grammar, offering rationales for new approaches that include classroom research and direct teaching of grammar generated by student writing. She discusses the need for teachers to learn grammar again—or for the first time—and includes sample lessons for teachers and students. (www.heinemann.com)

Zemelman, Steve and Harvey Daniels. *Writing Project: Training Teachers of Composition from Kindergarten to College*. Portsmouth, NH: Heinemann, 1985.

Internet Connections:

www.funbrain.com. *This educational site includes language arts games that are great practice for schoolchildren.*

www.grammarlady.com. *The Grammar Lady site is great for questions and reference help.*

www.iei.uiuc.edu/student_grammarsafari.html. *Intensive English Institute, University of Illinois at Urbana-Champaign.* Grammar Safari *is a fine resource for teachers and students. Includes games, lesson plans, research, practice pages that are educationally solid and enjoyable.*

www.ncte.org. *National Council of Teachers of English (NCTE). Check out the links for NCTE's Assembly for the Teaching of English Grammar.*

www.postdiluvian.org/~gilly/Schoolhouse_Rock/HTML/grammar/grammar.html. *Based on the seminal children's educational TV series* Schoolhouse Rock, *this site offers fun and educational ways to learn the basics.*